22
Landmark
Years

22 Landmark Years

Christian Schools International, 1943-65

John A. Vander Ark

Assisted by Gordon Oosterman

Baker Book House

Grand Rapids, Michigan 49506

ISBN: 0-8010-9291-4

Printed in the United States of America

Contents

Preface

Now this is eternal life: that they may know you, the only true God, and Jesus Christ, whom you have sent.

John 17:3, NIV

What is the chief and highest end of man? Man's chief and highest end is to glorify God, and fully to enjoy Him forever.

Westminster Catechism

Let every student be plainly instructed and earnestly pressed to consider well [that] the main end of his life and studies is to know God and Jesus Christ which is eternal life and therefore to lay Christ in the bottom as the only foundation of all sound knowledge and learning. . . .

Letter, September 26, 1642,
explaining the reason for
establishing Harvard College

These three statements, first expressed on different continents during different times, each express the essence of Christian education. The purpose of life and the purpose of learning are, at bottom, of one piece. Civilized societies have always acknowledged this.

The purposes of life and learning are essentially theological issues, and one's theology *is* important. Consequently people who take their faith seriously wish to entrust the education of their children to those of a similar faith. It was so with God's people in Old Testament times, in New Testament times, and has been ever since. Those committed to a faith other than Christianity evidence a parallel concern (witness the Jews, the Muslims, the

Hindus, and the Marxists). Within the Christian tradition this ongoing concern is most noticeably expressed institutionally among such diverse groups as Roman Catholics and Mennonites, Lutherans and Seventh-Day Adventists.

It should come as no surprise that the founders and the promoters of Christian schools that have been part of the fellowship of Christian Schools International, known for many years as the National Union of Christian Schools, also believe that life and learning belong together. Life and learning have purpose only when they reflect the purpose of Him who is the source of all life and meaning.

The distance between a goodly heritage and its extinction is but one short generation. The following account is an honest attempt to understand an important part of that heritage that connects us to the faith of our fathers and, more importantly, the God of our fathers. May it serve to enlighten and encourage all joined in the great work of Christian education as we share with the generations that shall follow us that indeed "the fear of the LORD is the beginning of wisdom, and the knowledge of the Holy One is understanding" (Prov. 9:10, NIV).

Acknowledgments

I am deeply grateful to several people who were especially involved in this project:

Gordon Oosterman, social studies consultant at Christian Schools International, helped plan a series of writings on Christian-school history, of which this is one. He critiqued my manuscript and composed certain pages.

Dorothy Wallinga skillfully typed the manuscript.

Linda Triemstra meticulously edited the manuscript.

Betty De Vries selected and placed the illustrations, and coordinated the production of the book.

To those who encouraged me to put in writing an account of persons and events in the unfolding of Christian-school history, and to those who responded to my requests for providing data and interpretation, I give a hearty thanks.

Special thanks to my wife, Julia, for her encouragement and forbearance with my preoccupation over the long haul in completing this project.

Prologue

Hear, O Israel: The LORD our God is one LORD; and you shall love the LORD your God with all your heart, and with all your soul, and with all your might. And these words which I command you this day shall be upon your heart; and you shall teach them diligently to your children, and shall talk of them when you sit in your house, and when you walk by the way, and when you lie down, and when you rise. And you shall bind them as a sign upon your hand, and they shall be as frontlets between your eyes. And you shall write them on the doorposts of your house and on your gates.

Deuteronomy 6:4 – 9, RSV

There are two kinds of people in the world: those who believe the Lord has spoken, as He has through Jesus Christ (Heb. 1:2), and those who do not. The goodly heritage is the one of faith in the God of the Scriptures. That this faith is first identified in the Old Testament and is amplified in the New is apparent to all versed in the literature of the Bible.

The implications of this fact, as they apply to education, appear frequently. The poetical books of Proverbs and Psalms are replete with references to remember the wonderful works of the Lord (Pss. 78, 136). Formal education as one thinks of it in our generation is quite unlike the arrangement by which a tradition was handed down in both Old Testament and New Testament times, but the purpose is clear: that the learners may come to know the Lord, His mighty acts, and His everlasting mercies. Occupational skills were not neglected, but were learned in the context of apprenticeship, as exemplified by Peter, Paul, and Jesus.

Patterns of early and modern Christian education emerged from Hebrew practices. In Elisha's time there were schools known by

9

the term *sons of the prophets*. These schools were guilds or broth-
erhoods for the training of prophets. From them some towering
individuals arose. The concept of family was always honored in
the Jewish tradition. Fathers taught their children the Torah and
the implications of the Shema, beginning at the fourth year. Although the origin of formal education is obscure, we know that
each synagogue was expected to have a school.

The early Christians, as Howard E. Kershner has pointed out,
would not send their children to the pagan schools of Rome, but
instead insisted on creating schools of their own. They also prepared for their children literature that recognized the true God,
Jesus Christ, and avoided all mention of the pagan gods.

Christians living during the days of the Roman Empire had a
difficult time. Periodically they were openly persecuted; frequently
they were criticized for not participating in the civil religion. In
the realm of formal learning they were heavily influenced by the
appealing yet pagan Greek model for learning that found wide
expression throughout the Roman Empire.

Following the political collapse of the Roman Empire in A.D.
476, Christians found themselves in an uncertain situation during
which the church of the time assumed most of the responsibility
for formal education. Its few schools had a heavy orientation toward service in the church. The barbarism of Europe was beset
with near anarchy; this was superseded by the development of the
feudal system, in which the church exercised a dominant role in
education. Occasionally special schools were set up as palace
schools, some of the most notable being those of the days of
Charlemagne (c. 800). These schools, however, complemented the
teachings of the faith; they did not oppose them. It was also during
this period of the Middle Ages that the universities began to appear, although the enrollment was small and their influence not
great.

Toward the end of the Middle Ages, however, in the wake of
the Crusades, and prior to the excitement of the Renaissance and
the pre-Reformational stirrings, education that concerned Christians was taking on a new character. The accretions of centuries
of tradition in the church and the church's educational practices
were being questioned and, by some, challenged. Others felt there
was a better way and that was to quietly set up schools that more
accurately manifested the purpose of Christian education at its

best. Among these in northwestern Europe were the schools of the Brethren of the Common Life, founded by Gerhard Groote about 1350. Groote and his followers hoped to bring about reform in the church by means of Christian education in which the teaching of the Bible would be preeminent. Among those who attended these schools were Erasmus and Thomas à Kempis.

The Reformation had a telling effect on education. The new wine of the Reformation, so to speak, would not be contained in the old skins of the monastic order. Martin Luther, accenting personal profession of faith, believed that the first provision of the Lord for Christian education is to be found in the priesthood of all believers. A consequence is that this principle indirectly encouraged people to become literate.

In *What's Lutheran in Education*, Allan H. Jahsmann summarized well Luther's ideas on education:

> But individual responsibilities, . . . are carried out formally through what he calls the natural orders: the home, the state, or community, and the church. Underlying Luther's philosophy of education is the premise that these natural orders are institutions appointed by God in the interest of man. Hence he and all those following him speak of the responsibility as well as the control of education as threefold.
>
> Luther and his followers have written a great deal about duties or obligations of parents and also about their rights and authority. On the basis of the creation account and other passages of Holy Scripture, they all agree that the basic institution for the teaching and training of children is the home or family, that parents, especially fathers, have the first responsibility for the education of their children, and that the teaching and training of children according to God's will is the highest responsibility of parenthood.[1]

Reference to the resurgence of Christian education in the Reformation would be wholly inadequate without mention of John Calvin's contribution. He, like Luther, fostered the principle of the priesthood of believers, and expanded on the teaching about the nature of God's revelation and its significance to Christian nurture. Calvin founded and operated Geneva Academy, which was the prototype of countless subsequent schools in several nations. With Jean Cordier as chief assistant headmaster and curriculum

1. (St. Louis: Concordia, 1960), pp. 24–25.

director, Calvin organized a school with well-defined objectives and practices. Through his pupils, Calvin's influence was spread in Europe and subsequently into America.

In the century following the Reformation, a modified system of Christian education developed in colonial America. The local government, particularly in influential New England, was a type of theocracy, with church and state interknit. Local autonomy had high priority, and was expressive of the belief in the priesthood of believers. A Calvinistic influence was noticeably evident in *The New England Primer*. Early in the 1600s, however, there were indications of change. Schools were by civil law made community schools (e.g., 1642 and 1647 in Massachusetts), with the inevitable result that schools reflected social and ecclesiastical conditions of the communities. Seeds of what eventually came to be known as public education were sown, the earliest change being that of compulsory school attendance.

On this point a caution must be sounded. "Public school historians," says an authority on the history of private schools, Otto F. Kraushaar, "often point to these and subsequent acts of the Massachusetts General Court as marking the beginning of the American public school system. That claim is not well substantiated."[2] The state that made those acts was an ecclesiastical as well as a civil state, one that brooked no religious or educational rivals. Hence, the town schools were similar to parochial schools, inasmuch as they were established and governed by quasi-ecclesiastical bodies.

To try to establish any significant connection between early American schools and contemporary Christian schools is a hazardous and speculative undertaking. Research is scanty, but it is obvious that there is no unbroken line. Private schools under the aegis of Presbyterian, Episcopal, Reformed, Methodist, and other churches flourished for a time as religious institutions, but many closed when "free" education was introduced. Some survived as prestigious, nonreligious schools, but most cannot be considered forerunners of contemporary Protestant Christian schools.

Throughout western Europe and Anglo-America the eighteenth century became increasingly secularized and became known as

2. *Private Schools: From the Puritans to the Present* (Bloomington, IN: The Phi Delta Kappa Educational Foundation, 1976), p. 10.

the Age of Enlightenment. "Knowledge is power" was the password. A Prussian concept of universal education was popularized to the point that government used education as a means to advance nationalism. This was in sharp contrast to the Reformation emphasis of promoting literacy for worship and for Christian service. In Anglo-America, a novel and revolutionary separation of church and state gradually developed. Growth of a secular spirit, deism as a dominant religion, immigration from diverse European countries, the growth of centralized government, and a host of vaguely "democratic" influences began economic and social changes that made it more difficult for Christian education to compete with tax-supported, "free" educational institutions.

Culturally sensitive people repeatedly stressed the importance of education. This concept became part of an emerging civil religion. An act of Congress in 1787 granted vast public lands in support of education. At that time the act did not really influence the issue of public versus private education, but in time it favored public education exclusively. The ideas of John Locke, a secular humanist (before the term was in common use), had a notable effect on influential men such as Thomas Jefferson and Benjamin Franklin; two counterparts in the late nineteenth and early twentieth centuries were Horace Mann and John Dewey.

During the late nineteenth century, the nation expanded industrially. As industrialization and urbanization became increasingly powerful factors, learning was further stripped of religious content. Suffice it to say here that the opportunities for family values (in contrast to the "practical" education openly shared on the family farm) to be transmitted directly to children were sharply curtailed in the less personalized situations of urban schools and urban life.

Secularism continued to gain ascendancy. Private schools increasingly became options only for those who could afford them. Philosophies of education emphasized equality of opportunity, resulting in a one-track curriculum and methods of teaching. There was a great concern for citizenship (*civitas mundi*) to the exclusion of the consciousness of the kingdom of God (*civitas dei*). Mann promoted the avowed ideal: publicly supported schools, attended by *all* children, as a means of developing values that all might share as part of a civic consciousness that was abetted by a civil religion.

The Canadian Christian schools, like many American Christian schools, came into existence nearly a century later. They also have at best a tenuous connection with the early independent and religious schools that stretch back to the colonial school. To understand the history of Canadian education one must remember the British North America (BNA) act, the constitution that confederated four existing provinces in 1867. Two school systems were in existence at that time — Protestant and Roman Catholic. The Protestant system succumbed gradually to secular influences. It became known as the public school and the Catholic system was called separate.

The history of schools associated with Christian Schools International (CSI) goes back to the end of the nineteenth century, but the origins of the schools go back to a European context of that century. The same is basically true of most of the Christian schools in the Lutheran and Roman Catholic fellowships, although each of these groups has a distinct history. Immigrant people of the Calvinistic tradition founded early Christian schools of the Presbyterian and Reformed heritage. These schools were not, first of all, visible protests against the developing political, philosophical, and religious influences that were changing the nature of American and Canadian education. They were a continuation of the conviction that children from Christian homes should be taught by Christian teachers for Christian service.

These Christian schools are direct descendants of Calvinism in the Netherlands in the nineteenth century. They arose under conditions that led to a secession from the established state church of the Netherlands in 1834. The weakening of historic orthodoxy in the state church was also reflected in the gradual exclusion of Christian influences in the schools of the state.

Denied the right of separate church and school organizations and victimized by economic and social pressures, those who seceded began emigrating to America in 1847 to find the freedom denied them in their homeland. Led by an advocate of distinctly Christian schools, Albertus Van Raalte, the movement in western Michigan did not win much public favor during the early years. These early schools of Dutch immigrants were parochial in the sense that they were directly governed and operated by the church. Their history largely paralleled the history of the Christian Reformed Church (CRC), which was organized in 1857. That the schools were parochial is attested by a resolution of an official ecclesiastical conference in 1870: "The elementary school is the nursery of the church. . . ."

In the early schools of this group, instruction was inferior, teachers poorly prepared, and equipment inadequate. Forced to eke a living from the wilderness, the settlers were not much interested in education. However, during the 1880s a Calvinistic revival, sparked by Groen Van Prinsterer and dynamically spread by Abraham Kuyper, swept the Netherlands. The new movement restated the Reformation ideals of the sovereignty of God and said the Christian must express his culture through, among other things, distinctly Christian institutions of learning. The new ideology stressed that education was the basic responsibility of the parents, not to be controlled by the state or the church. Kuyper gave to education a rationale in theology. Soon to follow was Herman Bavinck, who brought pedagogical insight not previously articulated in Reformed thinking.

A new wave of immigration in the 1880s and 1890s gave the Christian-school movement in the United States fresh impetus. Among the new immigrants were professionally trained teachers. With other educational leaders, they began to raise the quality of instruction and the standards for teachers, as well as improve facilities. In 1892, under the leadership of the Reverend Klaas Kuiper, several schools in western Michigan adopted a resolution stating that schools could be better maintained through parental associations than through parochial-school arrangements.

The effect was that between 1892 and 1920 many new schools were brought into existence as "society," not church, schools. All but a few of the existing schools opted to be free from direct church control. In 1892, at the meeting where the resolution was adopted, there was also a decision to form an association for mutual advice and cooperation. It was the Society for Christian Instruction on a Reformed Basis, and embraced about ten or twelve schools already in existence. The Michigan Alliance succeeded the original union, and other alliances soon came into being.[3]

3. Two sources on the meeting in 1892 are Henry Kuiper, *The NUCS Is Born* (Grand Rapids: NUCS, 1954), and Donald Oppewal, *The Roots of the Calvinistic Day School Movement*, Calvin College monograph series (Grand Rapids: Calvin College, 1963).

"In Union There Is Strength"

First logo of The National Union of Christian Schools.

Out of the Chicago Alliance, the National Union of Christian Schools (NUCS) came into existence on September 1, 1920. A committee of three principals — Andrew Blystra, Mark Fakkema, and Henry Kuiper — had been appointed to investigate certain problems regarding the education and financial welfare of teachers, teaching materials, and supervision of schools. The committee concluded that the problems in the Chicago Alliance were extant in all Christian schools and that cooperative action was necessary. The Chicago Alliance sent invitations to seventy-three Christian schools to send delegates to a proposed organizational meeting. Thirty-seven schools responded; eight with power to act voted to establish the NUCS at a meeting in the First Roseland (Chicago) Christian Reformed Church.

Early in the history of the NUCS, its leaders determined that the organization's function would be service rather than supervision or control. Under the enthusiastic leadership of its first executive officer, Fakkema, the movement grew, and with its growth the NUCS became a strengthening entity.

Meanwhile, public education from its inception in the 1830s and 1840s created problems for private education. Mann's grand design was to build a school system that would, in Kraushaar's words, "not only provide education in the secular subjects, but also would shape the minds with a religiously rooted common value system forming the bedrock of American republicanism. Mann, himself a practicing Unitarian, believed that the schools could instruct the young in religion without being sectarian."[4] That, of course, did not satisfy many families who believed in bringing up their children in the teachings and the implications of a particular faith.

Moreover, an attitude was being forged in the American citizen that the public school is one of the chief bulwarks of the republic. The origin of the expression *melting pot* is a passage in Israel

---

4. The word *sectarian* in this context refers to doctrinal peculiarity.

Zangwill's play, in which he gave blatant articulation to a bigoted notion that was to add to the problems of those of African and Asian origins, as well as Indians and those unwilling to fuse "the crescent [Islam] with the cross [Christianity]."

> America is God's Crucible, the great Melting-Pot where all the races of Europe [sic] are melting and re-forming! Here you stand, good folks, think I, when I see them at Ellis Island, here you stand in your fifty groups, with your fifty languages and histories, and your fifty blood hatreds and rivalries. But you won't be long like that, brothers, for these are the fires of God you've come to — these are the fires of God ... Germans and Frenchmen, Irishmen and Englishmen, Jews and Russians — into the Crucible with you all! God is making the American ... the real American has not yet arrived. He is only in the Crucible, I tell you — he will be the fusion of all races, perhaps the coming superman. ...
>
> Yes, East and West, and North and South, the palm and the pine, the pole and the equator, the crescent and the cross — how the great Alchemist melts and fuses them with his purging flame! Here shall they all unite to build the Republic of Man and the Kingdom of God ... what is the glory of Rome and Jerusalem ... compared with the glory of America. ...

The play ended with the "softened sounds of voices" singing "My Country, 'Tis of Thee."

Needless to say, those committed to Christian education, whatever their ecclesiastical or ethnic background, were not about to jump into the allegorical pot. At the same time, this sloganeering of a civil religion made available a handy weapon to assail the conerns and the allegiances of those presumably at variance with the mythical majority. Private and religious schools were made suspect and faced many obstacles. Attempts were made through legislation to curb and even outlaw them. In the famous Oregon case, *Pierce v. Society of Sisters* (1925), the United States Supreme Court firmly asserted that parents have a right to send their children to a school of their own choosing.

These years immediately following World War I were a significant period. In the wake of great tensions over what constituted a proper sense of patriotism among Reformed Christians, a greater spirit of nationalism emerged. By and large, patrons of Christian schools had, prior to World War I, vigorously maintained their cultural identity in America. After this war suspicion of minority groups increased in many states. As a result, legislatures began to tighten their school-attendance laws and raised the age levels at which youth must be in school. High-school enrollments soared and in communities where Christian elementary schools were in existence, pressure from without stimulated the development of Christian high schools or academies.

During this period, teacher education in Christian institutions of higher education had its beginnings among those in this heritage. In 1917 leaders involved in the Michigan Alliance organized a Christian Normal Society. Its program, however, was short-lived. Calvin College in Grand Rapids, Michigan, became a fully accredited college in 1920, as ideas on a teacher-training course under the preparatory school of Calvin College began to ferment. A few Christian secondary schools were promoted for their normal courses that prepared graduates for teaching in Christian elementary schools.

Because of such developments, and in spite of difficulties, the schools continued to grow. There were years when teacher shortages became acute. There were the years of the Depression when loyal teachers continued their work in spite of drastic reductions in salary and occasional failure of a board to pay even what little it had promised. Yet, in the new generation conviction was deeply rooted. There were, it is true, many Christians unconvinced that Christian education is a Christian obligation, but their alibis diminished as Christian schools showed themselves worthy of a place in the academic world. The burden of proof of their alleged incompetencies shifted to the unconvinced.

The period from 1920 to 1943 is a natural division in the history of Christian Schools International (CSI), as is the period from 1943 to 1965. From the beginning of a common concern through the organization of a unifying service institution and on through a time of drastic social and economic changes, the movement not only held its own, but also continued to grow.

Christians are exhorted not to be encumbered by needless baggage or distractions in order that they may "run with patience the race" of the Christian life. Immigrant groups inevitably abandon some of the cultural baggage with which they come to a new land. There is this notable difference in what is discarded, however, between those who consider their basic citizenship to be in their nations — either past or present — and those who consider their basic citizenship to be in the kingdom of God. For the latter their faith remains something *not* to be discarded. Their realization of how it has enriched and blessed their lives understandably causes them to want to share it with their children. This means of sharing includes formal education, the most powerful educational means ever devised by the mind of man.

This, in essence, is the heritage embodied in the history of CSI. This publication will deal with one period of its history, that of 1943 to 1965. We hope, the Lord willing, to share other periods of its history at a later date.

John A. Vander Ark
Grand Rapids, Michigan
1982

1

Forcing of Issues

Before one can talk intelligently about forcing of issues, one must have a clear sense of issues regarding Christian education that were dominant from 1943 to 1965. The issues were a mixture of forces in education: religion, promotion (philosophy), and structure (organization).

The Anglo-American Educational Scene

Had John Dewey assessed Christian education in the mid-forties, or at any time for that matter, he would not have liked what he saw. Christian schools have always been slow to make changes, in part because they are naturally conservative, traditional, and frequently poor — and changes do cost money. What is more, Christian educators hesitated partly because they didn't fully understand the dominant thoughts of the leading secular philosophers and the applications of their philosophies; they were especially wary of the notion that man and not God is the center of the universe.

Christian educators used the names of Dewey, William Heard Kilpatrick, Edward Thorndike, Boyd H. Bode, and others of their kind primarily in slogan fashion, with the intent to warn against and escape their influence. There were more important things to do than spend time and effort in examining and evaluating "progressive" views and their applications to the operation of schools.

Dewey's thoughts may be summarized in the words *experimentalism* and *social efficiency*. His ideas always seemed to challenge traditional concepts in philosophy and education. Kilpatrick, Dewey's star expounder, "encouraged a dichotomy between teaching children and teaching subjects, to the disadvantage of the acquisition of organized knowledge."[1]

In the 1940s the "cult of the child" was very much alive. A whole lexicon of terms from secular thinking fell on Christian educators: progressive education, changing the social order, child-centered education, the project method, 8 – R bonds, democracy as a way of life, and life-adjustment curricula. All pointed to a basic non-Christian assumption "that man is the measure of all things." This meant to modern educators that "morals originate in human experience and are validated in terms of their effects upon people."[2]

George S. Counts personified the thinking that a new social order was necessary. He advocated that teachers organize professionally, boldly reach for power, and use the schools to indoctrinate for the reconstruction of society. Like Horace Mann, who opposed what he called sectarian instruction in the public schools despite a predominantly Protestant society, Counts would have the schools continue to promote the tenets of a civil religion acceptable to all. Counts placed public educators in many predicaments by trying to implement his ideas.

From this new smorgasbord of educational dainties Christian educators refused to eat. They did not loosely swing with the fads of the unstable educational pendulum. Nonetheless they did implement some changes in their curricula, from a heavy accent on the tools of learning to subjects that prepared students for increased competency for life in the mid-twentieth century. To their credit they maintained a steady curriculum of conventional subjects for basic education. Christian educators, while not oblivious to contemporary concerns, maintained their own theory and practice and, in their estimation, had better things to do than dabble in untried theories. J. C. Lobbes, long-time teaching principal in Christian schools, explained better than most of his colleagues the familiar theme of the relation of general to special revelation. In an address entitled "School Branches [subjects] Viewed as Branches in the Tree of God's Self-Revelation," he stressed that creation in all of its dimensions is the rightful workshop for the Christian school.

1. V. T. Thayer, *Formative Ideas in American Education: From the Colonial Period to the Present* (New York and Toronto: Dodd, Mead, 1965), p. 253.

2. *Ibid.*, p. 244.

One other concern was gaining prominence among Christian educators by the mid-forties, namely, that both our teaching and learning must be conducive to the "integration of personality," a way of saying that a Christian should be a person of integrity. It is a kind of Christian alternative to the child-centered emphasis of progressive education. The aim of Christian education, argued Henry Schultze, is not amassing facts, acquiring a well-disciplined mind, or developing character, all worthy in themselves, but is restoring the image of God in the pupil, "throughly furnished unto all good works" (II Tim. 3:17, KJV).

Concerns of the Faith

With respect to religious and spiritual concerns among most public-school leaders in the mid-forties, religious neutralism and outright secularism seemed the only just causes of the public school. Despite their mouthings about the right of conscience and freedom of belief for all, in effect these educators promoted a lowest-common-denominator civil religion, a faith that was at best a counterfeit Christianity.

In Protestantism generally, this was the heyday of Karl Barth, Paul Tillich, and Reinhold Niebuhr. There was in Anglo-America, following World War II, not just a single or dominant theological issue that engaged thinkers. There was rather a creeping liberalism and a steady process of disintegration of traditional Christian beliefs and values. Evolution and progressive education — specifically, the attempts of some scholars to provide theological underpinnings for these theories — were perhaps the most dominant theological issues that Christian educators could address. Liberalism and neoorthodoxy were not simply matters of a distrust for the biblical account of creation and a substitution of another version of the origin of mankind, but also gave haven to a more subtle force, the idea of the innate goodness of man. The implications were becoming readily apparent in textbooks on the natural sciences, but also were evident in literature and social studies.

The Anglo-American ecclesiastical scene was colored, if not dominated, by the World Council of Churches, which was essentially an ecclesiastical United Nations. It represented primarily the theologically liberal churches. In protest to its claim to speak for all the churches, the National Association of Evangelicals (NAE) was formed, evidencing concerns for the defense and the promotion of the historic Christian faith.

Political Factors

There were strong implications for Christian education not only in the current religious milieu but also in manifest political issues. The lingering effects of the Depression were fading, as were recollections of World War II. The memory of how political climates can drastically and rapidly be changed, namely, the rise and the enormous power of Hitler and Mussolini, was picked up as valuable grist for educational mills. Counts had come out in 1932 with a widely-read pamphlet, "Dare the Schools Build a New Social Order?" The old dictum that schools should teach how to think, rather than teach only the mastery of tools of learning and many facts, had been put to a severe test in the totalitarian states. What were the implications for America if progressive education and its call for building a new society were to be taken seriously?

The issue of social planning was, of course, not restricted to the sphere of the school. As was demonstrated in Nazi Germany and Fascist Italy, social planning could mean tyrannical government control over all aspects of society. A perceptive contribution to literature about Christian schools is an address, "The Trend Toward State Socialism: A Threat to Our Schools." The title practically says it all. The Reverend Gerrit Hoeksema, who delivered this address at the 1945 convention, contended that the threat was real and the result would be inevitable control of the forces that determine the thinking of all citizens.

One must, of course, be careful not to assume that there were no contrasts between the 1930s and the 1950s in this regard. "The 30's were marked by a phenomenal increase in public school population and flexible adjustments in curricula in order to satisfy the alleged needs of young people for whom economic life no longer provided open opportunities."[3]

In the wake of World War II came new demands, a return to traditional values. The economy was strong and educational goals were not as restricted as formerly, when obtaining gainful employment was a major if not overriding concern. There were confusion and disillusionment, however. Schools and colleges were not providing either basic education or a sense of purpose in life and society in a technologically changing world.

3. *Ibid.*, p. 260.

Priorities Among Christian Schools

The implications of these issues were not lost on Christian educators. Responses, although basically from individuals, can be traced through institutional voices and pens. For many years promotion of Christian education centered on the themes of the covenant idea; the essential unity of the home, church, and school; criticism of public schools; and the structure of parent-controlled schools, all with the context of taking the Bible seriously.

Mark Fakkema.

Mark Fakkema expounded the themes regularly and forcefully in his office as general secretary of the National Union of Christian Schools (NUCS). Sometimes his patience with the body he addressed so often seemed to wear a bit thin. In the 1946 *Christian School Annual,* he complained that "the Covenantal basis of our Christian school movement is little more than an empty phrase with a large number of teachers." This was stated in the context of first giving a soft compliment to the teachers who stepped into the breach when the supply of qualified Christian college graduates was drastically short, but then decrying their preparation in public institutions. At this stage, Fakkema was beginning to structure his educational philosophy.

The Reverend Edward Heerema, the only person to hold a fulltime position as promotional secretary, from 1949 to 1953, analyzed these themes in "What School for Our Children?", a publication that is still widely used. In subsequent speeches and writings he examined various facets of the effort to defend and promote Christian education. One of the more dramatic themes was an answer to the question, Are Christian schools divisive? This issue stemmed from the erroneous concept that public education is a bulwark of American democracy. Spokesmen for secular education, such as James B. Conant, forthrightly suggested that the espousal of private education is dubious patriotism. The nub of Heerema's argument is that Conant's suggestion is spurious. The essence of our democracy is recognition and tolerance of its pluralistic character.

A Medium for Promotion

Christian Home and School has been the official magazine of the NUCS since March, 1922. A. S. De Jong was the editor, having been appointed to that position in 1937. He served in this capacity until 1947. For fourteen successive years (1924 – 1938) he also served as president of the NUCS. Educated in the Netherlands and a person of marked dignity, he brought that characteristic to bear on editing the magazine. Like his renowned predecessor, Garrett Heyns, who was editor from 1922 to 1937, De Jong was not a member of the NUCS office staff.

In 1946 Cornelius Zylstra was appointed editor for one year. Incidentally, he received a gratuity of twenty-five dollars per month for the professional service. In those years there was a popular demand to make the magazine more practical in terms of parental interest and teaching suggestions. To help effect such a change, Everett Kuizema was named chairman of the magazine committee. When John A. Van Bruggen was appointed educational director in 1947, the board decided that the editorship ought to be integrated with the directorship of the NUCS. Thus, Van Bruggen became editor of *Christian Home and School.* Other personnel soon became involved. Henry Kuiper was added to the magazine committee to bring teaching and administrative experience to it. To help make the magazine a more effective instrument, Beth Merizon was selected as associate editor. In 1953 the editorship fell on John A. Vander Ark, who became the executive officer.

All those who guided the destiny of the magazine struggled with the difficult assignment of appealing to a wide readership — teachers, principals, parents, board members, ministers, support-

CHRISTIAN
Home and School

● Time Out for Children   ● Cigarettes and the Heart
          ● Symbolism and the Christian Faith
● Rubbing Shoulders and Shaking Hands   October 1965

ers of all levels of maturity and education. With varying degrees of success, those responsible tried never to loose sight of the magazine's chief objective, namely, to bring before the Christian community the compelling claims of Christian education, which begins in the Christian home and continues in the Christian schools.

A Canadian Counterpart: The Christian School Herald

Christian Home and School, notwithstanding its principal objective, was not serving the Canadian constituency adequately. As late as 1957 many immigrants were still struggling with the English language. The NUCS received a few overtures from Canada to publish a Dutch section in *Christian Home and School.* Out of fear that such a provision would seriously reduce distribution in the United States, the NUCS did not honor such requests. In addition, many leaders in Canada felt the need for more content relevant to pioneer work in starting Christian schools.

To meet the local needs for promoting Christian education via the printed page, the Hamilton (Ontario) Christian School Society started a small publication early in 1957 called *Christian School Herald.* It used the Dutch language exclusively. The purposes were to present fundamentals of Christian education and establish Christian schools. The lead article in the third issue was "Waarom Christelijke Opvoeding?" ("Why Christian Education?") by the Reverend T. C. Van Kooten, a Christian Reformed pastor in Hamilton. One reader responded with a gift of one dollar, which he hoped would be the beginning of a strong fund for their own school paper — ". . . een zeer beschieden begin voor een heel groot, sterk fonds voor onze eigen schoolkrant."

The third issue, June, 1957, with the Reverend Adam Persenaire and Dick Farenhorst designated as editors, promoted Hamilton District Christian High. The goal of the Hamilton society was to serve a larger readership. By September the Ontario Alliance

Rev. Adam Persenaire.

(NUCS District 10) took the magazine under its auspices and revised its staff, making Persenaire chief editor, and Jennie Visser,
the Reverend W. Van Dijk, and Farenhorst co-editors. The alliance
immediately sought provincewide circulation, and later, nationwide distribution.

Masthead of
Christian School Herald.

Like *Christian Home and School, Christian School Herald* tried
to address the wide range of concerns of its constituency. Each
issue contained articles on basic principles, news, and encourage-
ments to developing societies and Christian schools.

The exclusive use of Dutch soon gave way to the language of
the land. Of significance is that by July-August, 1958, the original
Dutch article by Van Kooten was reprinted in English.

The benefit of having a magazine for the promotion of Christian
education was great. The editorial board of *Christian School Herald* also published three monographs between 1963–1965 for use
in discussion groups. Two were written by P. Y. De Jong. Sprinkled
in these monographs are names such as Persenaire, Praamsma,
Venema, Vander Pol, de Jager, Hart, and Tamminga, all of whom
contributed articles to the magazine. The third monograph is a
symposium on the distinct character of Christian education, gleaned
from past issues by teachers Visser, Charles Hoytema, Tom Abma,

Bernice Schrotenboer, Albertus (Bert) Witvoet, and student Gary Duthler.

As Canadian Christian schools increased in number, changes were made in both editorial staff and contents, not always to the complete satisfaction of readers. Debatable subjects were broached and pointedly differing opinions were freely printed. Articles concerning the cultural relevance of Christian education to the Canadian scene found a prominent place in the magazine. *Christian School Herald* continued with success in serving a timely need. Subsequently, in the 1971-1972 school year, it was phased out and a special arrangement was made with the NUCS to retain a Canadian contributing editor for *Christian Home and School* and provide for bulk distribution in Canada.

Promotion via the official organ of the NUCS, the *Christian Home and School*, continued unabated.

Salaries, Security, and the Economic Situation

The challenge of this period to implement something more with respect to the lordship of Christ and the serious business of bringing up children, would, without a doubt, have been harder to accept if the economic climate had not been favorable. In comparatively few years the situation changed drastically, to a point where the demand for goods and services could hardly be met. The war, however ruthless and destructive of life, property, and lifestyles, restored a degree of prosperity that made the support of private education more viable again. While contending with a shortage of building materials, Christian schools could be built anew or enlarged.

When the NUCS was launched in 1920, one of its programs was to improve and make more secure the economic position of teachers in Christian schools. That was an almost limitless and most difficult objective. Many papers and speeches about improving salaries and providing a pension plan were delivered. The history of the attempt to realize these goals is an account of valiant hope countered by repeated frustrations. In the 1920s, two concepts regarding financial security were generally promoted: annuities and a mutual benefit fund, a measure that would provide help for disability, death, and unusual needs, as well as retirement benefits. Prodded by the Chicago Alliance, in 1925 the NUCS adopted an unrefined plan combining the two concepts. Unfortunately nothing was developed.

It was not unusual to hear a discouraging and somewhat cynical answer to the question, "What must a Christian-school teacher do upon retirement?" The answer sometimes snidely given was, "He can always go to the deacons." The NUCS performed some surface-scratching acts in this period. For example, the board of directors in 1930 gave B. J. Bennink, who had lost his life's savings because of the Depression debacle in Western Academy, $10.00 per month from its general fund. The following year the NUCS established a fund for retired teachers. To provide for such a fund, schools were asked to contribute five cents per pupil annually. Regrettably, the good intention was short-lived. Bennink's dole was raised to $15.00 per month in 1940. Mrs. Frank Driesens, whose husband died in 1940, received $12.50 per month and authorization was needed bimonthly. Efforts, however, were not restricted to bail-out measures. Attempts were made in this early period to raise salaries. A recommended uniform salary standard was adopted in 1940. It provided beginning teachers who held a normal certificate with $900.00 per year, with annual increments of $25.00 up to sixteen years. Principals were to receive an additional $100.00 for each room for the first five rooms. Thereafter it was $25.00 per room.

The Pension Saga

In 1938 a mutual benefit, catch-all plan was approved at the annual meeting in Muskegon, Michigan, subject to ratification by three-fourths of all teachers and school boards. It was enthusiastically supported by all the alliances except the Michigan Alliance, which was still dominated by a self-sufficient spirit and a myopic view on national programs. After several modifications and promotion especially by the Eastern Alliance, one of the leaders in this area of concern, the Christian School Employees' Mutual Benefit Fund (CSEMBF) was adopted and went into effect in September, 1943. Benefits were in three categories: disablement, death, and superannuation — a term peculiar to the day, meaning pension. To provide necessary monies for the fund, the plan called for an assessment of 2 percent of the employee's salary, one-half of which was paid by the teacher or employee and one-half by the local board. The benefits were low; in fact, utterly austere. Superannuation benefits were, for example, $8 per each year of service. For a thirty-year tenure, a single teacher would receive an annual pension of $240. Married men would receive $480. For purposes of stabilizing the fund and to meet "unforeseen emergencies," a contingency fund of $25,000 was set up. The revenue for it would come from a nationwide campaign.

In order to avoid the problems of incorporation, the CSEMBF was replaced after only one year of operation by a better-conceived organization, the Christian School Pension Trust Fund, effective September, 1944. The original trustees continued as administrators of the new trust fund: G. B. Van Heyningen, president; Andrew Blystra, secretary; C. H. Ippel; Lambert Bere; and William Brouwer. All were from Chicagoland except Ippel and all were highly dedicated and eager to have the new plan become viable and accepted by the constituents. Blystra, as secretary and later as secretary-treasurer, has the distinction of being called the father of the pension plan.

The development of the contingency fund was quite an enterprise. A committee, consisting of W. J. Dykstra, chairman, Henry Denkema, and John Hendriksen, was appointed to collect $25,000. The enthusiastic work of the committee resulted in gathering nearly $60,000 by 1949, which served as an excellent psychological as well as financial hedge against the approximately $250,000 liability with which the pension plan was saddled at the outset, having assumed obligations for service for which no contributions had been made. (One must understand a feature of the pension plan that was important to the architects of the plan, but unheard of in actuarial circles: a retroactive component, giving pensions to all former Christian-school employees for whom no contributions had been made.)

Unfortunately a strain soon arose between the committee and the NUCS over the use of the monies in the contingency fund. The committee wished to have the pension fund's board of trustees and the NUCS board of directors make discretionary use of some funds in hardship cases. The administration chose to keep the contingency fund intact except for extreme emergency, such as the possibility of bailing out the pension fund in the event of another economic depression.

The tension was eased by the establishment in 1946 of yet another fund, the Christian School Employees' Temporary Relief

Fund. The purpose of this fund was to supplement payments to retirees whose pensions were inadequate to allow them to live with self-respect. It also was to provide funds for quasi-eligible persons not specifically covered by the pension trust fund. The sources of revenue were personal gifts and special church offerings when the pension fund became a cause accredited by the synod of the Christian Reformed Church (CRC). Many pensioners benefited from this fund from its inception.

The pension trust plan had a survival-tested career in its early years. Many school boards and noncareer teachers did not want to participate in the plan. Although the benefits gradually improved and there were attempts to provide a more equitable distribution of contributed monies, the plan was popular only among participants who were quite certain they would make a career of teaching. A one-time attempt to make school participation a requirement of membership in the NUCS failed dismally. The assumption that *all* Christian-school employees were interested in paying for the pension benefits of career teachers was dramatically repudiated by the resistance to contribute without a guarantee of tangible and equitable benefits to the contributors.

The plan nearly hit a boat-swamping storm in 1951 when employees of educational institutions were first permitted to participate in Social Security. (The Social Security Act of 1935 specifically forbade the participation of employees of private institutions. The bugaboo of separation of church and state hung like an albatross on political necks. Gradually, the concept prevailed that citizenship has only one class, not a first and a second. Opinions had been greatly divided among Christian-school people when joining was voluntary. There was some humor and irony in the fact that in the studies leading to the establishment of the pension plan, the term used for the private plan was "social security.")

The superiority of one system over the other — pension plan versus Social Security — was vociferously debated. Many school boards felt they could not afford to participate in both and chose the latter because of its transferability that would benefit those who would not remain in teaching. Unfortunately, at that time the idea that private pensions are a necessary supplement to Social Security was not prominent. For a few years the pension plan was hanging on the ropes. New life, however, was infused into it by

1963 Board of Trustees, Christian School Pension Trust Fund. L to r: Richard Schurman, James La Grand, Gerald Knol, Calvin Nagel, Richard Tolsma, William Brouwer, William Westveer, Dr. Robert Paxton, John Vander Ark.

increasing the contributions to 4 percent and slowly raising the benefits.

Leadership, both executive personnel and trustees, changed in the course of time. Vander Ark became the secretary-treasurer of the pension plan when he accepted the position as director of the NUCS in 1953. In 1957, Gerald Knol was appointed as business manager of the NUCS with accounting responsibilities in the pension fund; soon he was appointed its executive treasurer. With his fiscal expertise and a changing board of trustees, all of whom shot up their antennae to soak up signals from the constituency and also brought their own thoughts to bear, the pension plan steadily changed for the better. Terms such as *actuarial soundness* and concepts of the relationship of incoming contributions and outgoing benefits were not merely bandied about, but were put to work in amendments to the plan. Having a policy of advance funding in contrast to pay-as-you-go indeed proved to be wise in the light of meeting future regulations imposed on private pension plans by both the United States and Canadian governments. By 1961 the reserves reached a seemingly unfathomable figure of one million dollars. This had come both from payments from participants in the plan and through the judicious investment of existing funds. Professional counsel was obtained. The relationship of a participant's contribution and ultimate benefit was carefully considered. By 1963 the plan was completely restated and a successful image was established by 1965.

Salaries Upgraded

For many years salaries for teachers and principals in Christian schools were chronically inadequate. Almost all, especially those with families, were forced to take on summer employment in order to have a standard of living comparable to that of the typical constituent in the Christian-school community.

In 1963 the NUCS, in a now-familiar fashion of doing something about what its executive board judged to be good suggestions from its constituents, initiated a plus factor in teacher economics and issued its first report about a study of salaries to the annual meeting in August, 1964. The report explicated sound policies and practices with respect to the remuneration of teachers and principals; it also aimed at getting more uniformity among schools. The delegates to the annual meeting were so impressed with the report that they adopted a resolution asking the NUCS to update the report as factors changed, which meant preparing a new report annually.

The initial committee set a pattern of representation: from school boards, William Worst and Raymond Vander Laan; from teachers, William Selles and Robert Talsma; from principals, Harvey Ribbens and Mark Vander Ark; and from the NUCS, Philip Elve. Committee personnel, of course, changes, but the function continues uninterrupted to the present.

Group Insurance Introduced

The NUCS took another step in increasing financial security for personnel of member schools in the early 1960s. After years of debate about whether a group life and health insurance program administered by the NUCS was proper and feasible, the NUCS appointed a committee composed of Louis Van Ess, Robert Topp, and Knol to study the issue. The result was a program acceptable to the membership at the August, 1963, annual meeting. Delegates also accepted a master policy covering student accidents. The role of the NUCS with respect to providing a wide range of financial-security measures had been clarified and strengthened.

Professionalization

The struggle for greater professionalization of teachers in Christian schools coincided with every historical era in Christian education. The founders of the NUCS ascribed much importance to professional qualifications and conduct of teachers. That was, in fact, one of the chief objectives in founding the organization.

In article 3 of the original constitution, five of the eight subheadings had a bearing on the teaching profession. Thirty years later, at the 1950 convention, seven of twelve resolutions adopted by the membership concerned the professional status of teachers.

One of the primary steps taken to encourage greater professionalization was the organization of institutes for Christian teachers. Beginning with the 1940s, the following were in existence: Eastern Christian Teachers' Association, Midwest Christian Teachers' Association (resulting from a merger of the Chicago and Michigan associations in 1935), Western (Tri-State) Teachers' Institute, Pella Christian Teachers' Association, and the California Teachers' Institute. The last was very new, having been formed in 1942 at Singing Pines on the Rim of the World Drive — a mountaintop experience, no doubt.

Three other teacher associations came into being in this period. The Canadian Christian Teachers' Association of Ontario originated in 1954 with a membership of twenty-five, and now embraces more than five hundred. John A. Vander Ark, with colleague Sidney Dykstra, was present at the organizational meeting. It was in an upper room of the Strathroy (Ontario) Christian Reformed Church. A pioneering professional spirit was present despite circumstances of austerity. Having traveled many miles and having met for a few hours, the teachers present decided to break for lunch. The "statesiders" assumed that meant an interlude at a restaurant. Not so. Out came brown bags, and to nullify embarrassment of the unprepared guests, several Canadian teachers offered portions of their lunch to the nonplussed statesiders. That gesture may be considered symbolic of the sharing that prevailed concerning professional matters. The Pacific Northwest Christian Teachers' Association, embracing all teachers in NUCS District 7, originated in 1947. As schools developed in Alberta, the Alberta Christian Educators' Association was formed in 1962. The Florida teachers met as an institute in the early sixties without being formally organized.

These and other regional organizations of teachers and principals were and still are conducive to bolstering a spirit of professionalism among teachers and administrators. Their main agenda, however, is the staging of conventions and conferences that afford opportunity to share ideas, gain insights and, as a dividend, provide inspiration. In spite of these contributions, the teachers' associations did not satisfy the most provocative thinkers in the teaching ranks.

Voices in the wilderness cried for more tangible evidence of professionalization of Christian educators. One such voice and pen was that of Kuiper, one of the three main originators of the NUCS. In 1935 and again in 1950, he advocated a national association of Christian teachers on the grounds that it could be a complement to the NUCS that would spell out in its constitution an agenda for professional development. Teachers, moreover, had not been actively engaged in the work of the NUCS. Without a national organization, Kuiper argued, no one could speak or act for the profession.

Back in 1936, the Chicago Christian Teachers' Association went on record, influenced by Kuiper, who was from this region, as favoring a national association. However, when the Chicago group proposed the idea to the Midwest Christian Teachers' Association, it fell flat.

A substratum issue, always there, evidenced more outcroppings in the late 1940s, namely, the concern for a more articulate formulation of a philosophy of Christian education. This was related to rumblings for a professional organization and a journal. An influential spokesman and incisive writer on such matters was Cornelius Bontekoe, a teacher in Eastern Christian High. As contributing editor to *Christian Home and School* ("The time has come," the walrus said, "to speak of many things. ..."), he made a plea with cogent reasons for a professional journal. "Not only will a periodical prepare the way for an intelligent understanding of a philosophy of Christian education; it will be indispensible in applying it ... to every subject. ..."[4]

The Grand Rapids Educators' Club responded to these and other pleas. On November 15, 1950, it launched a small professional-interest sheet called *The Exchange.* John Brondsema, a West Side Christian School teacher, agreed to be editor. Dorothy Westra, Lambert Konyndyk, and Harold Kuiper assisted him. The subscription price was a modest one dollar, but only 325 teachers volunteered the fee. *The Exchange,* however promising, was short-lived. The production cost per issue was $150 and publication ceased unceremoniously in 1951.

4. *Christian Home and School,* January, 1950, p. 16.

That was not the end of the struggle to cultivate professionalization among teachers. The publishing of professional material was taken up by the magazine committee of *Christian Home and School.* Beginning in 1952 and continuing to 1966, the magazine fostered a department called Teachers' Exchange. It contained ideas on teaching, resource materials, and anything that stimulated professional growth. The department featured articles by staff and nonstaff members. In 1966 the feature was phased out and two pages took its place: The Teacher's Bookshelf and The Answer Center, both professionally oriented.

On the heels of failure of *The Exchange* another venture was added to the efforts to spur interest in a professional organization and journal. The issue at hand was the chronic shortage of teachers. In the process of recruiting teachers, the concept was broached that teachers themselves could steer youth into teaching and also raise the level of respect through a good professional spirit. In an address at the 1955 convention, William Radius offered the opinion that the entry of many teachers into the profession comes about through the inspiration to emulate a certain good teacher. Enthusiasm, delight in being a teacher, and professional competence are obviously basic to recruiting an adequate supply of teachers.

The NUCS pursued such pleas to increase in teachers a self-conscious professional image and to help overcome the chronic teacher shortage by encouraging and coordinating efforts to establish a professional organization of teachers. A large committee with G. Roderick Youngs as chairman and Dykstra as secretary reported that a professional organization "is necessary and desirable if the future of our schools is to be properly safeguarded and our growth stimulated."

The NUCS board supported the efforts of the committee and appointed a subcommittee to try to organize such an association.

Mastheads of *The Exchange* and
Christian Educators Journal.

Named were Youngs, Nicholas Yff, Dow Haan, Dick Van Beek, and John A. Vander Ark, who reported the idea that such an organization should be autonomous, distinctly Reformed, and as early as possible turned over to teachers. With the able assistance of J. L. De Beer of Calvin College, the committee composed a constitution and tried to implement a nationwide organization. District representatives were invited to an organizational meeting. The response was disheartening. However, seven representatives met in December, 1957, and formed what continues to be known as the Christian Educators Association (CEA).

It would be satisfying to report that the CEA became a bona fide, self-governing professional organization. Actually its membership is composed of regional teacher associations and education departments of Christian colleges. Dreams and realities are seldom identical.

After issuing several introductory *Newsletters*, CEA together with the education department of Calvin College published in the autumn of 1961 the first quarterly copy of *Christian Educators Journal (CEJ)*. Van Bruggen was editor and Yff was business manager. The editorial board consisted of representatives of CEA and Calvin College. The format was a sixteen-page, pocket-sized package. Calvin College and the NUCS subsidized the new journal. The Midwest Christian Teachers' Association was the first group to commit itself to the care and keeping of a forum to carry forward dialogues on Christian education. Within a few years other teacher organizations closed ranks, subscribed en masse, and assured the continuation of *CEJ*.

When this period closed, Donald Oppewal was serving as managing editor, a position he held with distinction for more than twelve years. Considering the exacting task of producing the *CEJ*, and that he often worked single-handedly, the constituency must appreciate his high idealism and sense of mission to promote the professionalization of Christian educators.

As the observer looks back, the obvious question arises, Did the times make the issues or did the issues make the times? Or to put the matter a bit differently, how much of what happened was beyond the control of even the best-intentioned and best-organized efforts? And how many good things were accomplished by committed, conscientious Christians who felt confident that the grace of God was their assurance and hope? Despite the disappointments, there is much to marvel about and for which to give thanks. As the partially-translatable Dutch expression has it, *Nooit Gedacht* ("Who would have thought so many good things have come to pass in so short a time?").

2

Temper of the Times

Church bells happily pealed out the news; so did blowing factory whistles and automobile horns as they honked crazily. People too excited to be mindful of who might be watching hugged one another in the streets out of sheer joy. In one community a hastily assembled group gave public thanks to God in the village park while a little boy, celebrating in his own way, noisily dragged a string of tin cans up and down the streets.

The date was September 2, 1945. The occasion was the official end of the fighting involved in the colossal slaughter known as World War II. For the United States it ended four years of intense preoccupation with winning the war. For Canada and the nations of Europe, as well as many parts of Asia, the war years had been even longer. To these could be added the uneasy years prior to 1939 when war clouds were gathering over Europe and the Far East. The emotional release that found expression this bright September day was thoroughly understandable. It was coupled with a fuzzy romantic notion that from here on all would be well. Everyone knew better, but it was a time for feeling, not for thinking. It was a happy occasion that few who experienced it can forget.

The early part of September is the traditional time for the opening of school doors for another season. Schools throughout Canada and the United States did open once again early that September, but students, teachers, and everyone else in society could scarcely realize the extent to which things would never be the same again. The end of World War II indeed was a pivotal point in the history of all the nations. Canada and the United States both would soon be caught up in extensive social and economic changes. Rapid urbanization was about to diminish the strong rural character of both nations. New inventions and technology, particularly in communication and transportation, would have a strong impact on home life and school. Changes for better or worse would become evident in the life of the church. But who would care to dream of or contemplate the impending sweeping changes on this "back-to-normal" September day?

Periods of history seldom have neat parameters. The ingredients of a period of history — issues, people, and events — generally come on the scene gradually, play their part for a spell, and then are reformulated or replaced without a sharp break. Toward the end of World War II the year 1943, however, signaled a dramatic change in the history of Christian schools.

That year marked the beginning of a time of phenomenal growth, and was a pivotal year for new developments in many phases of Christian education. Obviously, developments in the 1940s didn't spring into being apart from situations and thinking that were maturing in the immediately preceding years. An unprecedented prosperity, precipitated by World War II, replaced the worldwide economic depression of the 1930s. Parents were increasingly able to provide the financial means to build facilities for Christian education. Also of discernible significance were the massive demographic changes — larger families, immigration, and greater interaction of like-minded people — so that schools could be opened and operated.

Of utter importance was a new interest in the educational quality of Christian schools. Provocative questions were raised on the philosophy of Christian education and what it meant for the content, methodology, and teaching tools as expressed in courses of study, curriculum guides, and textbooks or manuals. Attendance increased not only at established schools, but overall enrollment also grew as new schools came into being. Canada saw its first school arise in Holland Marsh, Ontario, in 1943 under the quiet, effective leadership of Jacob (Uncle Bill) Uitvlugt. Two years later a school was set up in Lacombe, Alberta, and within the next two years Christian schools were operative in Vancouver, British Columbia, and Edmonton, Alberta, the northernmost of the great cities of the continent.

In the Philadelphia area a Christian school was organized by members of the Orthodox Presbyterian Church (OPC) in Willow

Grove, Pennsylvania, with Betty Blakemore as the first teacher. Soon a number of Christian schools were steadily developed within that denomination. Cornelius Van Til is credited with being the father of the Christian schools in the OPC, although due credit must also be given to J. Gresham Machen for his sterling addresses with respect to the movement.

Still one must return to the heartland of America (the upper Midwest) to examine the milieu that shaped the minds and events from 1943 to approximately 1965. In order to understand the postwar changes, it is necessary to summarize events that occurred during the two years before the end of World War II. Inescapable analytical questions arise. What was the faith commitment that gave rise to the rapid expansion in that period? What were the telling promotional activities that came into fruition? What role did the church, which mothered the movement and nourished it for approximately seventy-five years, play before and during the period? What was to be the effect of immigration after World War II, considering the fresh impetus immigration gave to the movement during the 1880s? What accounted for the new interest in Christian education among various Reformed, Presbyterian, and also non-Reformed fellowships?

Basic organizational problems of the Christian-school movement had been threshed out and quite well overcome between 1900 and 1930. The turning point toward parental, as distinct from parochial, schools was 1892. Attention soon after turned to matters such as the duties and the qualifications of school-board members. For example, it was suggested that the larger schools ought to divide their boards into standing functional committees with the principal as chief executive officer. It took many years for that idea to take hold and be reconciled with a strict interpretation of parent-controlled and the more prominent committee-of-the-whole concept of a board. Nevertheless, more school-board time was devoted to a consideration of promotional activities and to ideas other than merely "keeping schools." One example of more specialized functions of a school board is delineating the relationship between a school board and a consistory (the governing body of a congregation; it is comprised of elders and deacons elected from among the congregation).

It is a mistake to assume that the decade of the Depression had been merely a time for hanging on. True, some schools had to

suspend operation because money was not available, but most of
the schools held on by dogged determination and an avowed de-
pendence on God (the two are not incompatible). One may describe the time as testing years that brought convictions under
fire, but certainly not in a passive manner. Leaders promoted the
cause that they wholeheartedly considered nonnegotiable. The following remark reoccurs in the literature of the period and obliquely
chastises the makers of alibis: "In an affluent society it takes very
little conviction to send one's children to a Christian school."[1]

Mark Fakkema, more than any other individual, stood fast in
the promotion of Christian schools during the Depression. As the
executive officer — general secretary was his title — he used every
means available, including radio, the printed page, and mass meetings. He also worked on strengthening the position of the National
Union of Christian Schools (NUCS) among its member schools so
it received the appreciation it deserved.

The regional bodies, called alliances, also laid it on their school
boards to be more aggressive in promotion; "making propaganda"
was the popular term of the day. The Chicago Alliance proposed
that a number of school-board meetings each year should be used
for promotion. The Eastern Alliance advocated that eighth-grade
graduation exercises be introduced as a means of promoting the
Christian day school. Both the Michigan Alliance, which was highly
functional before the NUCS was organized in 1920, and the Western Alliance, which always had a large popular inner allegiance,
were tooled up for promoting the cause.

The board members of alliances were people of strong convictions, and so no one will be surprised to hear of disagreements
expressed in a manner other than gentle. The essence of one feud,
between the Michigan Alliance and the NUCS, was that the Michigan Alliance was doing for Michigan schools what the NUCS
proposed to do for all Christian schools. It printed the first year-
book, published the first magazine (*School Bell*), and prepared a
course of study and some instructional materials.

According to E. R. Post, long-time (forty-one years) principal of
Grand Rapids (Michigan) Christian High, western Michigan considered itself the heartland of Christian education. In their own
provincial way these people were concerned about the status of

---

1. *Christian School Annual*, 1944, p. 48.

their own schools and did not sense the need for a larger unity. For some time, skepticism regarding the benefit of interaction hampered the spirit of togetherness. Fortunately, the feud was pretty well settled by 1943, although vestiges remained for years to come.

Back in the Depression decade, a significant step was taken with respect to teacher associations. The Illinois and the Michigan associations in 1935 merged to become the well-known Midwest Christian Teachers Association which, as its main program, sponsored an annual teachers' convention and effectively induced teachers to broaden their horizons.[2] In time, teachers from Wisconsin, Indiana, New York, Ontario, and (for a while, on alternate years) New Jersey, were included. Gradually other regional associations were formed. These matters of an earlier decade provide the background for understanding developments from 1943 on.

World War II also had many influences on revitalizing Christian education. Primarily, it made leaders and patrons think about the current status of Christian education in a world clamoring for allegiances and the direction it should go. The theme of the annual convention in 1943 was "Our Schools in a World at War." Henry Schultze, then president of the NUCS board of directors, in an annual message to the churches, wrote, "... we shall have to fight to maintain our schools not only because of the teacher shortage that appears inevitable and not only because of the necessity of raising additional funds for an education, the cost of which is sure to go up, but primarily because of a lack of appreciation of the type of education our schools stand for. ... Christian education's interests go beyond the question: 'How can I earn a living?' It would solve the more important question: 'How can or must I live?' "[3]

Leonard Greenway, addressing the 1943 convention, boldly asserted that the Christian school is a bulwark against the demoralizing influences of war. Basically, the attitude prevailed that the war caused a resurgence in thinking on the value of one's character, morals, values, and life itself. It was indeed a time for reflection.

2. In 1976 the name was changed to Christian Educators Association (CEA).
3. *Christian School Annual*, 1943, p. 84.

Meanwhile an earlier challenge intensified. One of the biggest problems Christian schools faced during and after the war was a critical shortage of teachers. Enrollments increased, but the supply of teachers did not keep pace. There was, in fact, heavy attrition. Many of the men teachers were siphoned off into military service. Others were led into strategic employment where remuneration and financial security were much more promising.

It is not surprising, then, to realize that the economic well-being of teachers was brought into bold relief. Salaries, although still substandard, were raised and a pension plan was adopted after more than twenty years of flag-waving propaganda by the NUCS and several unsuccessful attempts to get something underway.

An interesting insight into a shortage of personnel is afforded us in the 1945 *Christian School Annual*. Principal C. Vos of a Roseland (Chicago) Christian school reported on a questionnaire prepared by a committee of principals and submitted to a cross section of schools. The questionnaire surveyed "setbacks in Christian schools on account of the war." The returns indicate that principals considered the greatest teacher shortage in the history of the Christian-school movement, especially the shortage of men teachers, as their bane.

Incidentally, Vos naively evidenced his thinking when he commented on the respective contributions of men and women teachers: "In the lower and intermediate grades it may well be that the latter are doing work that is superb, surpassing that of the men teachers. We do, however, believe that more men teachers are desirable from the point of view of developing a more balanced pupil, as well as a more stable system. The sterner and more resolute character of the man should leave its imprint upon the pupil as well as the gentler and more lovable character of the woman."[4]

Immigration

Immigration from the Netherlands stands out as a major factor contributing to the expansion of Christian education in this postwar period. To reliably tell the story of the growth of Christian schools, one must view the great demographic change in the Neth-

4. *Christian School Annual*, 1945, p. 73.

erlands. For many who emigrated after World War II, Christian
education was an ingrained way of life. Their concerns in education are paramount in this modern period, particularly in Canada.

Causes of the postwar exodus are complex and compelling. The
economic depression of the thirties was followed by the imposi-
tion of Nazism. By 1945 Holland had experienced five years of
systematic plundering by Hitler's hordes. Thousands of Dutch
workers were deported to Germany. Much of the fertile farmland
was inundated by salt water. Near-famine conditions existed in
the Dutch cities and many sensed the threat of a Communist take-
over as a stark reality.

Privations, the grim experiences of war, and an uncertain future
were all unsettling. So were schisms in the churches. A severe
housing shortage as well as the unavailability of farmland and a
seemingly suffocating bureaucracy plagued many people already
frustrated with high taxes and a military draft.

No wonder that many were disillusioned and willing to begin
a new life abroad. In the wake of personal, political, or financial
difficulties many energetic or desperate Dutch people were eager
for a new start. Understandably they were especially eager for
opportunities to provide their children with prospects for a more
abundant life, which they could not foresee in the homeland.[5] As
a means of relieving the housing shortage, unemployment, and
other severe problems, the Dutch government set up incentives
such as subsidies and services to increase emigration. Among the
larger nations, Canada offered great opportunities for the emigra-
tion-minded; Australia too, but to a lesser degree. The quota system of the United States was a curb to extensive immigration,
despite the words at the base of the Statue of Liberty: "Give me
your tired, your poor...." That immigration was a boon to the
Calvinist Christian school system in Anglo-America is a well-documented development that will be treated in more detail in a later
chapter. Christian education was a fixed cause in the Netherlands
and although the Canadian and American Christian educational
systems grew up quite independent of the Dutch system, the pe-

5. An excellent treatise on aspects of Dutch immigration to Canada and the
United States is by Gordon Oosterman et al., *To Find a Better Life: Aspects of
Dutch Immigration to Canada and the United States, 1920–1970* (Grand Rapids:
CSI, 1975).

riods of immigration show a marked influence on stimulating thinking on basic issues as well as obviously enlarging pupil population. One authority on Dutch immigration implied this point when he wrote: "Proportionately the Orthodox Calvinists contributed the most immigrants during the early postwar years. Although they constituted only 9.7 percent of the total population of the Netherlands in 1947, they made up 20 percent of the Hollanders who went to the United States during the period 1948–52."[6] Demographers have studied the reasons for emigration of this segment of the population with inconclusive results, but it can be said that the immigrants were a boon to the churches and Christian schools in Canada and the United States that shared corresponding commitments. In view of the fact that more Dutch immigrants settled in Canada than the United States, the churches and Christian schools in Canada predictably took on more of the color and the flavor of the institutions that existed in the Netherlands.

The process of incorporating the immigrants was markedly more rapid and complete than in earlier periods. Formerly immigrants settled in Dutch neighborhoods and retained their language and customs. The more recent Dutch immigrants were unusually successful in their newly adopted country, a circumstance that is attributed to their attitudes and abilities to learn the English language and to be contributing parties to Anglo-American culture. One must recognize also that higher educational attainments existed in the Netherlands than in previous generations; hence more skilled and professional people arrived.

Promotion

Bear in mind that the decade preceding this period of extensive growth was indeed a time of both intensive and extensive promotional activity. Two convention speeches at the 1947 convention give us some good insights on what was stressed. George Stob, speaking on the topic "Look to the Foundations," reminded his audience that we should never be satisfied with outward achievements, and expounded these assumptions. First is the simple sov-

6. Gerald F. De Jong, *The Dutch in America, 1609–1974* (Boston: Twayne, 1975), p. 186.

ereign fact of our relationship to God. Children, too, stand in that relationship to God—the covenant idea; therefore leading and training must be prominent. The public school, by its very nature, cannot foster education in that relationship because it is a conglomerate, having an attempted common-ground, humanistic foundation at best. The corollary is that the Christian school is an extension of and is governed by the standards of the Christian home. Therefore, the Christian school is built as it should be only by a thoroughgoing spirit of sacrifice by all involved in the covenant community.[7]

Another address, given by Richard Postma, president of the NUCS at that time, was entitled "Building for the Future."[8] He encapsulated what Christian-school leaders were thinking and trying to implement in various programs. God, not man, controls the destinies of the world and He reveals His divine plan to those who belong to Him. General revelation, Postma emphasized, must be seen in the light of special revelation. He, too, made direct reference to public education by calling the commonly accepted idea, a la Horace Mann, that the public schools might use a body of religious beliefs as a basis for fostering faith, a "futile hope." He decried the current terrifying problems with youth and challenged the Calvinistic Christian school movement with a twofold task. First, stress *back to God* in education and bring our message to fellow citizens. Second, show clearly the need for and implementation of good Christian education through competent teachers and well-prepared Christian textbooks. Both addresses are representative of the religious and educational values of the period as Christian-school advocates conceived them.

A chapter on the temper of the times would be incomplete without a clear reference to the incipient interest that arose among Christians with backgrounds other than in the Reformed and Presbyterian tradition. What accounts for the receptive attitude outside of traditional Christian-school circles? It sounds harsh to say, as Fakkema did, that "outside of our circles there is a great dearth of fundamental, coherent thinking touching things basic to life and the preparation to life and the preparation for life."[9] But that

7. *Christian School Annual*, 1947, p. 65.
8. *Ibid.*, p. 58.
9. *Christian School Annual*, 1946, p. 47.

is the testimony of many evangelicals who later saw the need for integrating faith and education. Doubtless the influence of the promotional activity of Fakkema, Schultze, Peter Eldersveld, and others extended beyond Reformed groups and encouraged a large segment of evangelicals to think about education and then act.

Acknowledgment should also be made of the steady influence of the denomination that is officially committed to the promotion and support of Christian schools, namely, the Christian Reformed Church (CRC). The CRC did not terminate or diminish efforts to promote the cause when the organization gravitated toward control by societies. The synods of 1932, 1934, and 1936 made official pronouncements with respect to the role of the church in encouraging Christian schools, particularly with respect to the indifference of certain ministers to the cause and to attitudinal qualifications of consistory members.

Thus, the milieu that shaped and reshaped Christian education in the 1940s was a sequence of dominant minds and major events. Given the conditions of the Depression, the subsequent return of prosperity owing largely to World War II, big demographic changes through higher birthrates and immigration, renewed (or revitalized) interest among the traditional (CRC) constituency, and a rising tide of interest among evangelical groups, Christian education as a truly fixed cause weathered the changing times. Better than that, it became stronger, in favor with man and God.

The temper that characterized the forties was the motivation for implementing programs in the fifties and sixties. It ushered in a consideration of issues germane to a growing system. For example, a call for a statement of philosophy was accompanied by the publication of textbooks and curriculum guides, which gave to Christian educational theory "concrete expressions in terms of curriculum content and practices."[10] Moreover, the spirit of the forties brought about a consideration of promotional priorities, reforms in administrative practices, and a better self-image.

---

10. Donald Oppewal, *Roots of the Calvinistic Day School Movement*, Calvin College monograph series (Grand Rapids: Calvin College, 1963), p. 37.

3

Developments Within the National Union of Christian Schools

$\mathbf{F}$rom its beginning, the National Union of Christian Schools (NUCS) has been a union of Christian-school societies. Membership in the union is by individual societies. However, regional bodies of Christian schools, called alliances, predated the NUCS. The four in existence in 1920 were the Chicago, Eastern, Michigan, and Western alliances. As schools developed in other areas, new alliances were formed: California, Dakota, Northwest, and Pella. (The Ontario Alliance was not brought into being during this period.)

Reorganization

Soon after the NUCS was operative, in 1924 a compromise was agreed upon to quell the misgivings of the Michigan Alliance regarding the alleged diminished role of alliances. A policy position was adopted whereby society membership in the NUCS would be continued, but representation at meetings would be through alliances. Members of the NUCS board of directors were nominated by alliances and elected at the annual meetings of the NUCS. The number of delegates and votes from each alliance was determined by the number of schools in its territory. In 1943, the Eastern Alliance, for example, was entitled to two delegates and five votes while the Michigan Alliance had eight delegates and twenty-two votes. NUCS board membership was also proportionate. (In 1940, delegates to annual meetings were paid three cents per mile plus one dollar for every four hundred miles for lodging and meals. Carpooling, understandably, was encouraged.)

The alliances in the early period generally maintained active programs, many of which helped to realize the objectives of the NUCS. There was some duplication of effort in the programs of the alliances and the NUCS, but none of major consequence.

In time the effectiveness of alliances began to weaken. There were practical problems. In some instances meetings were not scheduled; several isolated schools had no alliance to which they could belong; and often nominations for NUCS board membership were not made on time, if at all. But the greater issue was ideological. The idea that schools ought to have direct representation at annual meetings — a one-member-one-vote proposition — was gaining ascendancy.

In a proposal that foreshadowed the impact of Jacob Van't Hof, the future president of the NUCS board, the West Side Christian schools in Grand Rapids, Michigan, recommended a change. Van't Hof, a resident of the west side, was, at this time, the vice president of the NUCS board, and it is highly unlikely that this proposal was made without his full knowledge — and endorsement. He was that kind of a man. In essence, the proposal recommended a change in policy from representation through alliances to direct school-society representation in the NUCS structure. Directors were limited to serving two three-year terms. A committee consisting of Simon Dekker, Henry Schut, and Richard Postma was appointed to study the recommendation and report in 1945. They found that the school alliances were weak links in the system; the union was an organization of school societies, not alliances; there was need to bring the union and its member schools closer together; and decisions affecting schools would be better made by delegates from each school.

The issue of delegates at the annual meeting was debated with vigor; indirect representation decided upon in the early twenties

For many years this was the logo for the National Union of Christian Schools.

Jacob Van't Hof.

was changed in 1947 to direct representation. Alliances became NUCS districts. Not all constituents, however, were happy with the change. The effective date of the reorganization was to be 1949. Some alliances, for example, the Western Alliance, retained the word *alliance* and simply added the phrase *district 6*. The first all-Canadian district, consisting of the Ontario Christian schools, was organized in 1956, adopted the name *Ontario Alliance of Christian Schools*, and continues its use to the present. Representing Ontario was Lambert Huizingh from Holland Marsh, who had the distinction of being the first Canadian representative on the NUCS board. Two other Canadian districts were soon formed. Alberta (District 11) was established tentatively in 1955 and firmly in 1958. H. J. Ten Hove from Lacombe was the first to represent Alberta and Manitoba on the NUCS board. British Columbia (District 12), which was divided from the Pacific Northwest District 7 along the forty-ninth parallel, was organized in 1962. Syrt Wolters from Victoria was the first director from British Columbia.

To make the transition from alliances to districts more palatable, the NUCS prepared and distributed a paper entitled "A More Perfect Union" to all schools. This paper clarified the aims of districts and what the union intended to do for and with boards, teachers, principals, parent-teacher associations, and others. Implied in the reorganization plans was the expectation that the central office would have considerable control in planning district programs and meetings. The first district meeting planned mainly by NUCS personnel was held in District 6 at Rock Valley, Iowa. Van't Hof, John A. Van Bruggen, and the Reverend Edward Heerema were present from the NUCS office. The meeting was exceptionally well attended, but representatives from District 6 indicated they were not about to accept domination from headquarters. Other districts also stated their preference to plan their own agendas and, true to their heritage, many were unambiguously vocal about it.

NUCS Begets and Bids Adieu to the NACS

Mark Fakkema, general secretary of the NUCS, established a record of promoting Christian schools during the Depression and in years of prosperity. In one school year, for example, he gave 108 public lectures, one-half of which were in communities previously unfamiliar with the Christian school systems as identified by the NUCS. In addition, he wrote many articles and pamphlets and gave eleven radio addresses.

Fakkema personified the tension with which the NUCS wrestled for many years, namely, a concern for preservation of its heritage and also a desire to share convictions and insights with others. At this time in their history, Christian schools were being established at an unprecedented rate. The NUCS became identified as a rallying point. Ten new schools were added to NUCS membership in 1946, five in traditional communities (Arcadia, California; Oskaloosa and Wellsburg, Iowa; Grant, Michigan; and West Sayville, New York) and five in new outposts that heretofore held little hope of having Christian schools (Boston; Bridgeton, Vineland, and West Collingswood, New Jersey; and Seattle).

Fakkema had contacts with influential evangelical leaders and inveighed upon them to participate in conferences and rallies. L. R. Marston, bishop of the Free Methodist Church and president of its commission on Christian education, addressed the NUCS convention in Pella, Iowa, in 1946.

It became clear that with many evangelicals from various denominations seeking to start Christian schools, a new type of organization was needed. The NUCS could hardly consistently embrace all Christian schools within its Reformed and Presbyterian confessions and ideal of parent- and society-operated schools.

Two questions stood out in sharp relief. First, what kind of general doctrinal agreement or statement of faith would be acceptable to the body of sundry new schools? Second, what should be the nature of the organization? Should it parallel the NUCS or should it be an umbrella organization that would cover the NUCS and other national Protestant bodies?

Other crucial questions were these: How shall the NUCS fulfill its obligations and capitalize on the present opportunities? Can it absorb those it influenced without changing its basis? Will they be satisfied to be identified with the NUCS? Under Fakkema's influence the directors felt it was their duty to help form a new organization "or the present increase in Christian schools might prove to be as temporary as the Presbyterian Christian school movements in the preceding century."[1] The NUCS board seemed to favor cooperating with an overall organization, primarily, however, in order to *promote* Christian education.

Involvement in forming such an organization required authorization from the schools, in keeping with the constitution and bylaws of the NUCS. A resolution originating in the board of directors was adopted at the 1946 annual meeting in Pella and assigned to the board for action. Fakkema was authorized to bring the board's proposal to the National Association of Evangelicals (NAE) convention at Omaha, Nebraska, on April 14 – 17, 1947. The fact that the Christian Reformed Church (CRC) was at that time a member of the NAE was a plus for favorable action.

Fakkema effectively presented the proposal and the NAE board unanimously favored establishing a commission on Christian schools, stating that "the plan is to embrace all Christian educational institutions of elementary and secondary level throughout the country." Fakkema was asked if he would serve as educational director of the new organization, which was named the National Association of Christian Schools (NACS).

Before making a decision on the appointment, Fakkema knew that the relationship of the NUCS to the NACS had to be resolved. Some distinctly heated discussions took place. Evan Observant, the pen name for Cornelius Zylstra, editor of *Christian Home and*

1. Comments of the general secretary in the annual reports, 1946. This was obviously a reference to the Presbyterian churches' efforts to set up a system of parochial schools that began in 1845 and ended in failure about 1890 because of a lack of interest.

School (I've blown his cover after thirty-five years of immunity) stated that if the original plan materialized, the NUCS would become an affiliate of the NACS. The Illinois influence on the NUCS board, particularly that of Andrew Blystra and Fakkema, favored such an arrangement. The Michigan influence, which was waxing while the Illinois influence was waning, was not enthusiastic about that possibility. The proposal was stalemated. An option to change the name of the NUCS to include the term *Reformed* or *Calvinistic* was examined. This option implied having two completely separate organizations and different turfs for the promotion of Christian schools.

It was unfortunate that the issue had not been settled before authorization was given to Fakkema to promote the concept of a new organization to the NAE. Whatever was in Fakkema's mind on this point apparently was not conveyed unequivocally to the board. Accusations of misrepresentation were made, but not sustained. Evidently it was a case of one's enthusiasm overshadowing deliberate processes of the board regarding the consequences to the parent organization. Subsequent history reveals that the relationship of the two organizations was friendly and cooperative, but each maintained a separate identity. The NAE statement on faith, which is printed in appendix A, was adopted as the unifying doctrinal position of the NACS.

Fakkema continued to devote a large portion of his time to the promotion of NUCS work.[2] Meanwhile, Zylstra was appointed as the first educational secretary, but considering the necessity of moving to Chicago, he declined the appointment. Then Van Bruggen, principal at Oakdale Christian School in Grand Rapids, was offered the position. Apparently he had misgivings about working under Fakkema, the general secretary (i.e., chief executive officer), and declined. The board then decided to abolish the position of general secretary, designated Fakkema's position as that of promotion secretary, and persuaded Van Bruggen to be educational director and the chief executive officer.

In the light of that decision, Fakkema informed the board of

2. In the chapter on curriculum I will detail the established need for an educational secretary to handle the editing and publishing of Christian textbooks. Just enough on developments and new staff appointments made will be presented here to place in perspective the story of Fakkema's last year at the NUCS and his subsequent service.

the NUCS that he would accept the offer to be the director of the NACS. He placed two conditions on his acceptance. First, he wanted assurance that he could continue to promote Christian education on a Reformed basis, as he had done for twenty-one years with the NUCS. Enoch Dyrness, president of the NACS, answered, "That is what we expect you to do." Second, he requested that the NACS be an autonomous affiliate, not a commission, of the NAE, having its own board and raising its own finances. This, too, was graciously granted.

Fakkema's leave-taking from the NUCS was not as pleasant as one would like to report. He pointed out in the NUCS board meeting of August, 1947, that various churches (mostly Christian Reformed) had collected considerable sums of money to provide for promotional work both within and without Reformed circles. He stated that with the establishment of the new organization, promotional work outside of Reformed circles was coming to an end for the NUCS. He firmly stated, "You ought to give a dowry to the NACS." The board at first did not agree.

Fakkema then proposed a sabbatical year with full pay, having served "three times seven years." The board registered a tie vote. The tie did not really present a true picture of the board's appreciation or lack of it, simply because some of Fakkema's friends voted against the request in order to induce him to stay. Postma, president of the board, broke the tie in the affirmative, thus making possible a gift to the NACS in the magnitude of a full year's salary and a pension for its first executive officer.

Fakkema distinguished himself at the NACS in the same energetic, self-sacrificing manner as he had at the NUCS. He seldom took a vacation or indulged in recreation.

Relationships between the NUCS and the NACS were polite. It took time for the union to win the confidence of many of Fakkema's friends and generous supporters. In fact, some affluent persons who held him in high esteem continued to support him in his every undertaking. There was also much confusion in the area of church support, as consistories were not always able to distinguish between the two or decide which organization they meant to support.

The NACS flourished, as evidenced by the steady accretion of schools to its membership. Fakkema worked unceasingly to generate unity in the diverse body of evangelicals and especially to present to the constituents a world and life view that was different from the child-evangelism concept that many harbored.

Cooperation with the NACS had always been the aim and the desire of the NUCS board, and for the most part, there was mutual understanding and appreciation of one another. The union board, however, had certain reservations on factors that set limits on cooperation. These were spelled out at a meeting of the two boards, at the invitation of the NUCS, on April 27, 1950. The NUCS warned against entering into any relationship that would jeopardize or weaken its Reformed witness in its educational program, stated unequivocally that it could not help the NACS financially beyond the first year, and took strong exception to the constitutional provision of the NACS, which carried the clear implication that it should be spokesman for all Christian schools in America.

Disagreements within the NACS board over basic issues of Christian-school operation led to the termination of Fakkema's tenure in 1961. His remark fifteen years earlier foreshadowed the kind of differences that seemed bound to arise: "The truth of the matter is that many evangelical groups have no biblical view of life regarding various school subjects."[3] Then, too, there were clashes that stemmed from differences in personality and views on administration. Being accustomed to getting things done his way, Fakkema, it was reported, grew impatient with assertive board members.

But that was not the end of his service to Christian education. A coterie of his friends, among whom were Gilbert Den Dulk, Frederick Niemeyer, and John Van Mouwerink, assisted him in forming a new organization, the Christian School Service, Inc. Under the aegis of that private movement (no schools were members), Fakkema continued valiantly to promote Christian education. He published a journal, *Christian School Life;* issued many promotional pieces; and lectured on the philosophy of Christian education in hundreds of forums, among them Christian colleges. Christian day schools were as yet an alien entity to many of these colleges. In his lectures, Fakkema attempted to show that God is central in all phases of educational endeavor, ranging from basic principles to methodology. His accent was on moral discipline.

John F. Blanchard, Jr., succeeded Fakkema as the executive

3. *Christian School Annual,* 1946, p. 52.

secretary of NACS. Under his refined, Christian scholarly leadership, the organization enlarged its influence among evangelicals. The relationships with the NUCS were well defined and amiable. The house organ, *The Christian Teacher*, developed into a significant promotional and educational tool for the agency.

However successful Blanchard's career with the NACS, he became disenchanted with certain policies and practices of the NAE in administering the NACS, its affiliate. The NAE showed a lack of understanding of the needs of the NACS. For example, directors were appointed who did not patronize Christian schools by sending their children when the opportunities were there. Blanchard chose to return to Christian-school administration, selecting Portland, Oregon, as the place for implementing his cherished ideas.[4]

Headquarters Moved

The NUCS's first office was for many years in the house of Fakkema in Chicago. In 1941 office space was rented in Chicago at 11005 ½ South Michigan Avenue, and in 1946 additional space was secured at another site. Property was also purchased on Ninety-fifth Street and plans were being made in 1947 to erect an administration building there in Chicago, which was centrally located in terms of NUCS schools at that time.

Meanwhile, the effect of reorganization was beginning to be felt. Prior to 1945 all members of the executive committee were from Illinois. That year Henry Schultze of Calvin College was elected president. The other members were from Illinois: Blystra, vice president; Nicholas Yff, secretary; and Anthony Meeter, treasurer. In 1946 the complexion changed. Three executive committee members from Michigan were elected: Postma, president; Van't Hof, vice president; and John R. Bos, secretary. Thomas Stob of Cicero, Illinois, the treasurer, was the only officer from outside of Michigan. This marked the beginning of the label *The Michigan Influence*.

To compound the problem, in 1947, when alliances were replaced by districts, Illinois lost two of the fourteen board mem-

4. Although the subsequent history of the NACS is beyond this period, it is with sadness that one must add that in 1978 the NACS felt obligated to disband.

bers, because in actual practice the schools not affiliated with any alliance almost always selected their delegates from Illinois.

The editorial office that handled both the magazine *Christian Home and School* and Christian textbooks was already in Grand Rapids, since Zylstra and Van Bruggen were successively appointed as editors. Although Blystra had recently been appointed office administrator in the Chicago office, in 1948 the NUCS decided to move its headquarters to Grand Rapids, a decision that seemed inappropriate to the Chicago constituency. The reasons given for moving to Grand Rapids were that it would be cheaper to print materials there, the business and editorial function could be consolidated, it would be in the geographical area of the greatest density of the Christian schools, and it would be near to Calvin College. Needless to say, there was no jubilation in the city that cradled the NUCS for twenty-eight years. Chicagoland felt politically victimized.

On April 1, 1948, the move was made, first to 543 Eastern Avenue, a site recently abandoned by the Christian Reformed board of missions; then to another temporary location at 260 Jefferson Avenue. Lots comprising nearly two acres were soon purchased between Twenty-eighth Street and Everglade for the reasonable price of $7,527.52. Soon the board got plans underway to construct a functional administrative building there. These plans were integrated with the founding of the Christian School Educational Foundation (CSEF), whose primary objective would be to provide funds for the Christian-textbook program. An extensive financial campaign brought in $124,000, approximately $60,000 of which was an outright gift to the NUCS to give it a debt-free base of operation. The ceremony of laying the cornerstone was held on August 6, 1949; the new building was occupied in November. The building at 865 Twenty-eighth Street was expanded twice to meet the growing demand for more services and personnel, once in 1963 and in 1972.[5]

As the NUCS was settling into its new location and the expanded program began to require more revenue, the board decided not to increase membership fees but to turn to another

5. NUCS soon outgrew the facilities. In 1979, the completely renovated East Paris Christian School building became the home of Christian Schools International (CSI), the newly-chosen name for NUCS.

1945 Board of Directors of the National Union of Christian Schools

Standing l to r: R. Postma, (Grand Rapids, Mich.), J. Hendriksen (Kalamazoo, Mich.), J. Ten Harmsel (Hull, Ia.), H. Hugen (Pella, Ia.), W. C. Kooiman (Rock Valley, Ia.), J. Last (Passaic, N.J.), R. Zimmer (Redlands, Calif.), C. Aue (Orange City, Ia.), H. Schut (Hudsonville, Mich.).

Seated: T. J. Stob (Cicero, Ill.), A. Meeter (Lansing, Ill.), H. Schultze (Grand Rapids, Mich.), A. Blystra (Chicago, Ill.), N. Yff (Lansing, Ill.), M. Fakkema (General Secretary).

Note: Mr. Hoving (Lynden, Wash.) and Mr. Vander Veen (Corsica. S.D.) were not present.

Entrance to NUCS
offices at
865 28th Street.

mode of collecting additional monies. It set up a new position in
1950 and appointed Jerry Rozema as field representative. His tenure in that capacity was sadly brief, owing to a permanent disability caused by a paralyzing tumor. He was succeeded by George
Vander Zaag, who had remarkably similar credentials. Both men
had been successful in the food-selling business, had zeal for
Christian education, possessed the gift of meeting people, and felt
the urge to serve the cause they loved. This mode of gathering
funds, however, was short-lived. In 1956 the board reassessed the
method of obtaining funds and opted for mail campaigns, thus
abolishing the position of the field representative.

Teacher Shortage and Recruitment

In the literature of Christian-school operations, especially in
reports to the NUCS annual meetings, no subject except possibly
finance recurs more often than that of the problem of teacher
shortage. The language in the official publications was often plain-
tive, calling the problem a "chronic ailment," a "pernicious shortage of teachers." Frequently reporters or commentators suggested
reasons for the problem. The increase in enrollment and the establishment of new schools intensified the problem. Substandard
salaries were also obvious reasons. Sometimes spokesmen gave

some exhortative note such as "Our schools must have the best personnel," but were silent or brief about how to attain this commendable goal. Almost always they indicated that some form of recruitment was utterly necessary (a safe thing to say).

The call for more teachers was clearly sounded in 1945, following the crucial period during which teachers had been siphoned off from teaching duties for military service and strategic wartime jobs; others simply left for better-paying jobs. This exodus of teachers continued for the next two decades.

Schultze, president of the NUCS board of directors from 1938 to 1946, delivered a persuasive address about the shortage of teachers in what he called his swan song at the 1946 convention in Pella. In his inimitable way he bore to the heart of the alarming situation: "It is, of course, the part of wisdom to determine as accurately as possible the causes for the situation before we can prescribe any remedy."[6] He went on to list the major causes: inadequate salaries, lack of promotional opportunities, lack of professional status or spirit, and social insecurity.

Schultze then tackled the remedy: making working conditions more acceptable and launching a long-range recruitment plan as "the best means of solving the problem." Although he didn't make a separate point of showing the relationship of shortage to teacher preparation, he implied a strong correlation between adequate preparation and length of service. Interestingly, just two years later, the Grosse Point (Detroit) Christian Reformed Church gave one thousand dollars to the NUCS "to stimulate teacher preparation." Van Bruggen, executive director at the time, accomplished that objective through conferences for teachers in service.

The NUCS set up a formal recruitment program in 1953 with a small committee of five, Henry J. Kuiper, Garrett Keuning, Van Bruggen, Sidney Dykstra, and John A. Vander Ark. This committee laid a foundation for a long-range resolution as well as gave thought to meeting the immediate needs. The recruitment effort received a big boost in 1954 in response to a resolution adopted at the convention in Rochester, New York. A new committee of ten designed a multilateral program that used the printed page and personal appearances, formed high-school clubs for future teachers, and of great importance, established a special fund for grants and

6. *Christian School Annual*, p. 57.

loans to prospective teachers. NUCS sought the cooperation of many churches for two reasons: to gather money and to recommend prospective teachers. The committee proceeded in the spirit of one of John Calvin's disciples, John Sturm, who is reported as saying, "Give us wood and we will send you back arrows."

Over the years a great deal of money was distributed to aspiring teachers through the Teacher Education Assistance Fund (TEAF). Teacher recruitment was extensively advanced. For several years an NUCS-appointed committee, the teacher-recruitment committee, gave $250 awards or loans (often one person received two awards) to Christian college students who intended to teach in Christian schools.

While recruitment was going on, several smaller schools became discouraged by the problems all Christian schools face and in a sense were victims of the teacher shortage. Among those that closed were Dispatch, Kansas, in 1954 and Cleveland (East), Ohio, and Kenosha, Wisconsin, in 1956. As late as 1960, Monsey, New York, suspended its operation for similar reasons. Less dramatic but starkly disappointing was that many schools, especially in Canada, had to postpone the day of opening their doors because of an inadequate supply of teachers. An example was the John Calvin Christian School Society of Guelph, Ontario, which experienced such a disappointment in 1960 and had to postpone opening its school for a year.

Convinced that recruitment was most effective if administered close to home, some of the NUCS districts, particularly the Canadian districts, conducted financial-assistantship programs of their own. The teacher shortage was more acute in Canada, owing to the rapid increase in Christian schools and an almost nonexistent reservoir of prepared teachers. During the fifties and into the sixties, enrollment in Canadian Christian schools increased impressively. In 1951 a record was set, an increase of 75 percent. For the next nine years the average increase was 35 percent. The teacher shortage was truly a crisis. Attending college was expensive; in many instances the cost was prohibitive, since immigrant families especially experienced a dilemma. To send a son or a daughter away to school increased family expenses greatly and decreased the income that was essential to meet the family's needs during resettlement.

One example of many efforts made to appeal to young people

was a letter that Huizingh submitted to the *Calvinist Contact*. In it he challenged the talented to consider teaching as a profession and acquainted them with the subsidy program that the Ontario Alliance was ready to introduce. This was March 25, 1956. The crisis continued despite responses. The Reverend Adam Persenaire, in an editorial in *Christian School Herald*, March-April, 1960, called the issue "Our Most Urgent Need."[7]

In the United States, as in Canada, there was a strong conviction that local communities ought to provide at least as many teachers as they needed, although not all teachers would remain in their home communities. To stimulate that practice, the NUCS conducted a survey on this subject, specifically asking teachers who were currently teaching in Christian schools which church they considered their home church. Churches in rural and small towns provided many more teachers in proportion to local need than did city churches. The First Christian Reformed churches of Manhattan, Montana, and Hull, Iowa, were the leaders, each with twenty-two teachers claiming it as their home church.

The formal teacher-recruitment program did an immeasurable amount of good. In the United States, between 1954 and 1972, a staggering figure of approximately $250,000 had been received from church offerings and individual donations. This spoke well of the commitment to Christian education by those who themselves were not in a position to teach. By 1965, 820 prospective teachers had received grants or loans. Unfortunately, corresponding figures for those years are not available in Canada. The amount of money collected and distributed to help prospective teachers there was considerable.

Looking beyond these decades, one can report that the need to recruit teachers began to subside in the late sixties. Instead of a dearth, an oversupply was becoming evident. Certain prospective teachers still in college, however, were in dire need of financial help. Thus, between 1966 and 1972, forty emergency loans were made. In 1972 the teacher-recruitment committee was deactivated because it had fulfilled its original purpose. Since there was still

7. Gleaned from the unpublished paper (written for a course at Calvin College) by William Hoogland, "The Development of Calvinistic Christian Day Schools in Canada, 1943–1965," 1981.

some TEAF money remaining, the board authorized its use for undergraduate teacher scholarships.

The teacher-recruitment program was one service that terminated. In this period, however, several other services were introduced and continued as regular functions of the NUCS. Always high on the list of priorities was the establishment of new schools. In an increasingly complex society, Christian schools faced many problems and the task of the NUCS increased in its scope.

Services to schools were accomplished in a variety of ways. One method may be called a clearing-house function. An example of this category is the teacher-placement service through which the NUCS brought needy schools in touch with available teachers. A second category of service might be labeled advisory. Schools asking for specific help in promotional, financial, or other operational problems were provided with advice. A third kind of service was administrative. A prime example of this was the pension trust plan and fund, where the NUCS was charged with administering the plan. A fourth variety of service rendered was one in which the accent was on self-evaluation. Standards and model policies were made available for the local school to adopt or adapt for its use.

A major effort was also directed toward developing a distinctive philosophy of education and Christ-centered curriculum materials to enhance learning and teaching in the Christian day school. To get to that story, a verbal picture of the remarkable growth of the system between 1943 and 1965 will first be presented.

4

Growth

Among the Frisians common wisdom has it that a son should know at least as much and preferably more than his father. The leaders of the Christian-school movement at this time may not have been aware of such folklore, but surely they needed as much or more insight and commitment as their fathers had possessed to cope with the new set of challenges.

Factors That Encouraged Growth

As indicated in preceding chapters, the Christian-school movement embraced by the National Union of Christian Schools (NUCS) struggled for years to establish itself as a quality educational movement. Coming soon were an adequate supply of qualified teachers, greatly improved facilities, additional refinement of Christian educational theory and practice, and a more consistent quality in administration.

The early forties were a time of unprecedented growth. Grow the system did, not only in the number of schools and pupils, but also in facing and resolving many of the recurring problems. By 1943 the war-induced economic climate was favorable for the growth of Christian schools. Farm prices were at a peak and crops generally were good. Opportunities for labor in industrial communities were plentiful and wages were at record-breaking highs. In addition, students were spending more years in school, a fact that resulted in marked increases in the number of students.

At the same time, there was a cumulative effect of ideological differences throughout American education; Canada's situation was similar. Secularization was becoming more and more evident in the public schools as the theories of progressive education became practiced in the forties. Many startled parents opted for Christian schools, while others with long-held convictions on the purpose of Christian education now found themselves with the financial resources to effect their cherished goals.

The Annual Growth Table (Table 1) and the related chart (Fig. 1) present a graphic picture. (The list of new schools [Appendix B] according to years of origin provides additional information.) A few comments on Figure 1 particularly will reinforce an awareness of the rapid growth. Using 1943 as the base year, one notices that enrollment nearly doubled during the next ten years. In sixteen years it tripled, and by 1965, enrollment nearly quadrupled.

Encouragement and optimism took over where discouragement and frustration had previously been too common. The Hanford, California, Christian School Society, for example, opened its school in January, 1944. A short time before, the society concluded that having a Christian school was a hopeless dream. In desperation born of that assessment, it decided to bequeath to the NUCS whatever financial assets it had accumulated. In spite of the severest test of the time, namely, the shortage of teachers, the school opened. James Veltkamp was the first teacher-principal. In September the enrollment climbed to sixty-six and Gertrude Jansen was engaged as a second teacher.

Another example of renewed enthusiasm was in Leighton, Iowa. Having fallen on hard times, the Christian school had closed more than twenty years before. In 1943 it reopened with twenty-four pupils; Evalina Van Gorp was the teacher.

At the beginning of this decade the first such school in Canada opened at Holland Marsh, Ontario. Contrary to popular belief, this sizable expanse of productive muckland located thirty-five miles northwest of Toronto was not named by the Dutch settlers of this century. Rather it was named in 1790 after Sir Thomas Holland, a surveyor employed by the government at the time. Early settlers in this part of Ontario by-passed this swampy area in favor of other land that could be more readily cultivated. By the 1920s the government contemplated putting this marshy area to productive use and, realizing that farmers in the Netherlands had considerable experience in working such land, encouraged those with

Table 1
Annual Growth Table

Sept. of	Pupils	Increase	Percentage of Increase*	Number of Schools
1943	15,604	815	5.5	94
1944	16,970	1,340	8.5	99
1945	18,448	1,474	8.5	108
1946	19,837	1,389	7.5	115
1947	21,503	1,666	8.4	126**
1948	22,570	1,598	7.6	125
1949	23,970	1,400	6.2	133
1950	25,025	1,155	4.4	141
1951	26,651	1,526	6.5	156
1952	28,608	1,957	7.3	158
1953	30,768	2,161	7.4	167
1954	33,377	2,609	8.4	177
1955	35,793	2,416	7.2	187
1956	37,499	1,706	4.7	196
1957	40,754	3,255	8.7	207
1958	42,980	2,226	5.5	221
1959	45,641	2,661	6.2	231
1960	47,437	1,796	3.9	236
1961	49,570	2,133	4.5	246
1962	52,835	3,265	6.6	252
1963	55,192	2,357	4.4	256
1964	57,036	1,844	3.3	268
1965	59,535	2,499	4.3	277

*N.B.: The percentage of increase is not as reliable as actual figures

$$1957 - 3,255 = 8.7\%$$
$$1962 - 3,265 = 6.6\%$$

**There are some slight discrepancies in the figures reported. Prior to 1948 several schools were included which, although they were served by the NUCS, officially were not members. The reason for not affiliating basically was a philosophic difference. Also, increases do not always reflect the exact number of new schools. Some "administrative units" were added to original schools.

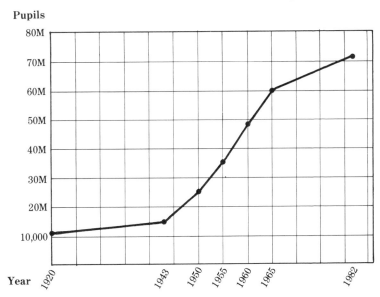

Figure 1
Increase in Numbers of Christian-school Pupils

needed skills to immigrate. A large dike was placed around the marsh, the water drained off, and what would prove to be a highly successful vegetable "patch" began. The region subsequently became one of the most productive in all Ontario.

The settlers in Holland Marsh were not typical and yet were harbingers of the type of immigrants who would be coming in the years following World War II. Coinciding with this development was a virtually worldwide economic depression that began in the late 1920s and extended well into the 1930s. The first Dutch immigrants who settled in the Marsh were among those who, rather than standing in line for handouts during the Great Depression, energetically reclaimed the seven thousand acres of fertile muckland. This land had been allowed to revert, after earlier sporadic attempts at farming, to a near-wilderness. First the people needed homes (perhaps the word *shelters* would be more suitable). Then, having formed a church and in quick succession a Christian-school society, the people were led and encouarged by the Reverend

Christian School at Holland Marsh, Ontario.   Jacob Uitvlugt.

Martin Schans. At an annual picnic, and remember this was a
Dutch-style church picnic, members of the society spontaneously
conceived the idea of having a drive for a school. Donations and
pledges from the thirty families totaled two thousand dollars,
enough to get a school underway. The now-acknowledged founding father of Christian education in Canada, Jacob Uitvlugt, became the teacher-principal, on February 15, 1943, of nineteen pupils
in eight grades. They were housed in an enlarged consistory room,
measuring twenty feet by twenty feet. The heating stove had to
be included also. Thus a new chapter of the Christian-school
movement was introduced. "It is," writes William Hoogland in an
unpublished paper, "more than just a chapter. It is really a story
in itself: a Canadian story about Dutch immigrants who struggled
to continue their tradition of Christian day schools, a tradition
rooted in 'the struggle for the soul of the child.' "[1]

Growth continued as the order of the day in the United States
also. In 1944 the garage of the parsonage of the Ontario, California,
Christian Reformed Church was remodeled to provide school-
rooms. The following year the city health and fire department
condemned this makeshift arrangement. Undaunted by such news,

1. "The Development of Calvinistic Christian Day Schools in Canada,
1943–1965," (1981), p. 1.

the school board (after a fervent prayer session) decided to build a modest school in which Principal A. C. Boerkoel could teach the pupils. One other California school was started in 1944, Alameda, in the Bay area. The first teacher-principal here was G. J. Boerman.

Significantly, two schools — Willow Grove and Middletown, Pennsylvania — whose constituents were predominantly of the Orthodox Presbyterian Church (OPC), were organized in 1943 and 1944 respectively. They were harbingers of that denomination's greater involvement in the movement. Schools with such constituency were organized in Bridgeport, Vineland, and West Collingswood (Camden County) New Jersey, as well as in Kirkwood, Germantown, and Pittsburgh (Wilkinsburg), Pennsylvania. Further west, members of this denomination were very prominent in establishing and maintaining a Christian school at Oostburg, Wisconsin.

At this time enrollments began to increase as much as 8.5 percent in a single year; this trend continued with minor exceptions every year to 1965. Again, see the Annual Growth Table (p. 69). The year 1947 is significant because the rate of growth was 8.4 percent more than that of the preceding year, even though seven schools whose relationship to the NUCS had been tenuous at best had terminated their memberships. These were Christian schools in Boston; Wheaton, Illinois; Potomac Association, Washington, D.C.; Philadelphia (Northeast); Corpus Christi, Texas; Seattle; and one in Denver. There had been differences in background and purpose that came to a point in differences with the confessional standards held by the NUCS.

The strength of Christian schools sometimes was manifest in ways other than increased enrollments. Several schools paid off their mortgages at this time. Eastern Christian High, for example, having been in operation for twenty-five years, burned an old mortgage in 1944 and began looking forward to better facilities. Incidentally, guest speakers at chapel keenly recall the devotion of students who, for want of proper assembly space, stood, not sat, for chapel four mornings each week for many years.

Building programs launched in 1948–1949 were typical of others during this period. Almost without exception old buildings that characterized nearly every school were renovated; many were replaced by new structures. Fifteen new school buildings were dedicated during this school year and work was begun on eleven

more. Reasons for the new or improved buildings were found in
a mixture of motives. On the negative side there was some desire
to "move up in the world" of physical facilities, to impress the
community, and — to the credit of no one — a bit of pride. On the
positive side there was a strong desire to meet an obvious need
and exercise good stewardship in the spirit of Nehemiah, who
challenged his fellow believers to rise and build. School societies
began rebuilding the outward manifestations of the kingdom of
God, which is, of course, in the hearts of those committed to Him;
many of these momuments of faith still stand and are in use.

Three Canadian Christian schools in addition to Holland Marsh
came into existence in the 1940s: Lacombe, Alberta, in 1945 and
Edmonton, Alberta, and Vancouver, British Columbia, in 1949. The
constituencies of all four were essentially Dutch immigrants who
were members of Christian Reformed churches. Lacombe acquired a one-room pioneer-looking building but was compelled
also to use the church basement to accommodate a rapidly growing school under the tutelage of Alida and Jenny Keegstra. Problems ranged from janitorial services to transportation in severely
cold weather to the antics of the older boys in dislocating the
outhouses, but all these were eventually overcome.

The advance scout of the movement in Edmonton was the Reverend Paul DeKoekkoek, who blazed a trail with Christian schools
in every pastorate he had on both sides of the border. He was
more than a leader; he was a strong advocate of good causes. In
Edmonton, while he was ministering to a congregation that had
an influx of immigrants, he initiated a monthly paper called *Canadian Calvinist*. This oriented readers to the Christian Reformed Church (CRC) as well as provided a vital promotion piece
for Christian education.

DeKoekkoek personified the militant leadership that held that
the CRC expected a positive response to article 41 (formerly article 21) of the church order: "The Consistories shall see to it that
there are good Christian schools in which parents have their children instructed according to the demands of the covenant."

The term *covenant* was used to describe the special relationship existing between God and believers. The word refers to a
bond that demands an active response to God in all of life. Children of believers are included in the covenant and therefore their

education is to incorporate a response to God in the learning process.[2]

The first Christian school in Edmonton was housed in the basement of a church, with Wilma Bouma teaching grades three, four, and five. A wooden school was built in 1951 for a two-room operation. An unexpected enrollment of 115 popped up, necessitating finding a third teacher. By 1952 there were 200 children whose parents were clamoring for their admission. The school board, under its president, the Reverend John Hanenburg, wrestled with many problems of developing school policies in the context of compounded adjustments for the immigrants. By 1965 Edmonton was a full (kindergarten through twelfth grade) consolidated system with three schools.

The story of Vancouver may not be as dramatic as that of Edmonton, but as the first Christian school formed in British Columbia and on the westernmost fringe of the new immigration, it was strategic. As was the case in Edmonton, the initiative to revive a dormant Christian-school society begun in 1944 came from the people who founded the church in 1927. The names of the Bonhof and Radstack families surface as leaders in the cause. Of particular interest is that the organizational meeting was held in a Presbyterian church, some of whose members were potential participants in founding a Christian school. This fact was indicative of the interdenominational nature of the school. School began during the fall of 1949 in a six-room house with an acre of land. Eighteen pupils in grades one through six attended. Miss B. Thompson was the first teacher. A new building was dedicated in 1951.

Unique among Christian schools is one in Neerlandia, Alberta. Having failed to start a Christian school in a settlement where nearly all the children were Christian Reformed or Canadian Reformed and attended the one public school, the people ran this school like a Christian school, selecting Reformed Christians as teachers and using NUCS Bible and other curriculum materials. Over the years these people have advertised for teachers in the *Banner,* a publication of the Christian Reformed Church.

An important historical footnote ought to be made at this point. The development of early Christian schools in Canada as well as

2. *Ibid.*, p. 4.

in the United States parallels the history of the Christian Reformed Church, which since its beginning in 1857 was indirectly responsible for bringing many Christian schools into existence. The Christian Reformed churches in Canada, prior to World War II, had a poor track record for establishing Christian schools. There are identifiable explanations, such as distances, poverty, lack of leadership, and small numbers; yet the fact of virtually no Christian schools is not easy to understand in view of the strong confessional backgrounds of most of these immigrants. By 1947 there were fourteen churches with an average membership of fewer than forty families per church; hence size has been proposed as an alibi. In addition some vocal parties claimed they wanted to be "good Canadians" and therefore wanted to patronize the Canadian public schools that supposedly were "not bad," were sensitive to religious values, and showed "a shadow of Christianity."

A conundrum to Christian-school historians is that the larger churches composed of the older immigrants, for example, in Chatham, Hamilton, Sarnia, and Windsor, did not organize schools until the newer immigrants became a part of the scene. Hamilton, which had a society already in 1937, did not organize a school until 1952. It must be noted, however, that an attempt to open a school in 1944 failed owing to the inability to find a teacher. The Windsor community did not organize a school until 1976. The mixture of immigrants of different periods caused problems and frustrations that needed a degree of resolution before cooperation became more commonplace.

NUCS Sees the Challenge

Throughout the development of Christian education in Canada the NUCS pursued the objective of being a promotional agency as well as a service organization. In 1952 the Reverend Edward Heerema, in his capacity of promotional secretary, voiced the high hope for vigorous growth of Christian schools in Canada. Quoting K. Norel in *Trouw* of December 1, 1951, he wrote, *"Onz volk in Canada roept om Christelijke scholen"* ("Our people in Canada are calling for Christian schools"). He made an extensive promotional tour of all communities that he thought held promise for development. His hope was based on the understanding that most

of the immigrants he addressed "were serious about matters of
principle (*beginsel*)."[3]

Consistent with the purposes of Heerema's tour, the NUCS
viewed Canada as a "promising field" and tried with varying success to serve the needs of a potentially burgeoning system of new
Christian schools. However, the new immigrants in Canada, particularly those from the Netherlands, were partially bewildered by
their new situations and needed time to sort through and work
out their priorities. There were highly noticeable changes in language, customs, laws, climate, and even in the system of weights
and measures. (The Netherlands at that time was on the metric
system while Canada was not.) The ecclesiastical situation in the
Netherlands had no direct counterpart in Canada, causing more
disorientation, and at least equally significant was that the Canadian government did not fund nonpublic school systems. In the
Netherlands both the public and nonpublic school systems, in-

Rev. Heerema stresses a point as Dr. Van Bruggen listens appreciatively.

3. *Christian Home and School*, July-August, 1952, p. 12.

cluding the Christian school systems, had equitable government funding. This practice was unknown among Canadians and even the idea was not appreciated by government officials. Consequently, support for Christian schools had to come directly from the pockets of the parents and others who supported Christian schools.[4]

What is more, the involvement of a United States organization in an already complicated binational, bicultural situation was neither fully understood nor always appreciated, even if the motives may have been purely altruistic (which they rarely are as people deal with one another). Well-intentioned actions can be soured by patronizing attitudes, something that Americans and particularly American Christians should have been more fully aware of years ago.

Regrettably, many Americans have not been as sensitive to Canadian identity and nationalism as they might have been. One Canadian member of the NUCS board of directors worded his complaint this way: "It is annoying to hear 'we Americans' so often." Another Canadian board member, however, did not share this sensitivity and in an early discussion on dropping the word *national* from the name *National Union of Christian Schools*, said, "The term *national* does not annoy me. I caution against dropping it." The issue was not posed as a confrontation, but differing opinions smoldered for several years. Finally, twenty-five years later the name was changed, dropping the word *national*.

NUCS District 10 was formed in 1952 with Heerema's help under the name *Ontario Alliance of Christian Schools*. This reflected both the widely accepted amalgam of existing Christian schools and an implicit reservation about being wholly absorbed by the United States-based organization.

Growth continued at an accelerated pace after 1952. The first of the new schools had become operational and served as models, at least in part, for even newer schools. Besides wrestling with the problem of acculturation, the immigrant families faced the reality of financing Christian schools and acquiring teachers. In many settlements there was also the question of what ought to be

4. For more details of the immigrants' experiences, see Gordon Oosterman et al., *To Find a Better Life: Aspects of Dutch Immigration to Canada and the United States, 1920–1970* (Grand Rapids: CSI, 1975).

provided first, a place to worship or a school. Some opted for a church building first, which delayed the opening of a school. New Westminster (now the Burnaby campus of the John Knox Christian School in urban Vancouver, British Columbia) evidently led the way to a viable solution to the problem. The Christian school was designed and built in 1955 with movable walls so that it might easily be converted into a place of worship. Victoria, on Vancouver Island, had a similar arrangement. It is difficult to pinpoint who thought of the idea, but it is generally agreed that the Reverend Henry Van Andel, an ardent spokesman for Christian education and sometime member of the NUCS board of directors, influenced its implementation.

Duncan, British Columbia, first used the social-activities room of the local church for a school. Eventually a separate school building was built on the church parking lot. With continued growth a larger site was purchased and in 1980 the entire school building was moved several blocks away to the new location. The Dundas (Ontario) Christian School was first allowed the use of rooms at the back of the church. These are but a few examples of sharing facilities in order to get a school started.

Some Christian-school advocates, however, strongly opposed sharing facilities with a church or even building a school on or near its location for the reason that the school would be thought of in the neighborhood as a parochial or provincial "Dutch" school. Immigrants, quite generally, feared that other Canadians would perceive the Christian schools as having isolationist tendencies and thereby supposedly hostile to the new land to which they had come as immigrants. Hoogland's research brings out that to counteract these impressions care was exercised in the choice of a name for Christian schools;[5] the name of Calvin or John Knox, his contemporary, was frequently chosen. Such a choice would be acceptable to the Calvinistic (Kuyperian) community, and would emphasize the Christian heritage and de-emphasize the Dutch ethnicity of those who established the school. In at least one community, Woodstock, Ontario, local officials discouraged or prohibited the use of the name *Woodstock Christian School* lest it imply that the existing public schools were not Christian. The supporters of the Christian school decided on the name *John Knox*

5. "Calvinistic Christian Day Schools," p. 15.

Christian School, for in their nation the third largest identifiable ethnic group is Scottish.

In Woodstock the school is close to the First Christian Reformed Church. A site for a church had been purchased, but before building even began it was recognized as too small to serve the rapidly growing fellowship. About that time the new route 401 had been completed and odd-shaped parcels of land adjacent to the highway were being sold to the highest bidders. Second-guessing what others might offer, the group bid a few dollars more than its competitor and bought acreage more than adequate for both church and Christian school. Some surplus land was later sold to a commercial enterprise; this reduced the land debt considerably. The city put in a new street to accommodate the school and without consulting the school patrons named it Juliana Drive, apparently a gesture of affection for the Dutch queen who spent the war years in Canada. Sometimes it seemed as though those trying to shed a Dutch image simply could not win.

A fine school and church were built on opposite ends of the property, and for some years the basement of the church doubled as a youth hostel in the summer. In August, 1979, both buildings were demolished by a tornado; subsequently both institutions have put up even better buildings.

The challenge of suitable buildings and the image they projected remained. In some instances, especially in the United States, there were a few planned efforts to bring the church and school into proximity, even sharing the facilities. Dearborn, Michigan, is an example of church and school built as one unit in 1957. The intent not only was economy, but also projecting a sharper image of the kind of school it wished to be.

Expansion Continued

The remarkable growth that began in the 1940s continued at an unprecedented pace throughout the 1950s to the mid-1960s. By 1952 there were in Canada 5 schools and thirty societies working toward having schools. At that time there were 151 schools in the United States and forty-one societies working with existing schools or toward establishing new schools. Come 1965 the number of schools in Canada increased to 61, with twenty-seven societies without schools as yet; in the United States there were 217 schools in operation and fourteen additional societies.

The year 1955 stands out in this history because it marks the beginning of Christian schools in the deep South, Ft. Lauderdale, Florida, being the first in the NUCS fellowship. The Christian Reformed Church for a century did not have as much as a toehold in the South. Members of the Orthodox Presbyterian Church, particularly the Reverend Donald Taws, must be credited with the foresight to establish a Christian school. Loraine Honadel pioneered as the first teacher-administrator. Both denominations used the availability of a Christian school as a means to induce people to take up residence and to expand the membership of their churches. Unfortunately, control of the school by one or the other denominational group in this community became a competitive issue. By dint of greater numbers and aggressiveness, the Christian Reformed constituency gained control. Fortunately that was not a serious deterrent to further cooperative action. Within ten years Christian schools in the NUCS fellowship were established in Lake Worth, Miami, Bradenton, Tampa, West Orlando, and St. Petersburg, Florida; Huntsville, Alabama; Memphis, Tennessee; and Shreveport, Louisiana.

By 1957 the high post-World-War-II birthrate was affecting the enrollment in elementary schools, giving the system a new record of 40,754 pupils enrolled; 3,255 were added that year, an 8.7 percent increase. The greatest gain in enrollment, 3,265 pupils, was in 1962; this was slightly more than the previous record in 1957. This gain was a surprise in the face of increased costs, slackened immigration, and the loss of several schools through closing or shifting membership to the National Association of Christian Schools (NACS). The greatest growth in one year within Canada was in 1962, when seven schools were added. The year 1958 went down in the annals with the distinction that no school in operation in 1957 failed to open its doors in 1958.

For Whom Are Christian Schools?

Although it is as old as the system, the question regarding the primary criterion for pupil selection came into prominence again in 1946 at the annual convention in Pella, Iowa. Mark Fakkema's predilection to recognize non-Reformed evangelicals was evident in the selection of personnel for the convention program that year. The keynote speaker was Bishop L. R. Marston of the Free Methodist Church. He and the clinics — discussion groups of ministers, teachers, board members, and principals — addressed themselves to the issue of admitting "outside" students. (The term was not intended as an opprobrium. It was an unrefined commonplace term casually used by the traditional constituency to identify those pupils and their families who were other than the culturally and ecclesiastically homogeneous majority.)

The ministers' clinic at the 1946 convention offered a resolution that would place well-guarded restrictions on the admission of outside students, particularly those from unchurched homes. The reason given was that covenant Christian schools are not evangelistic projects. The need for further thinking about this challenge was obvious to all. Christianity and Christian education are good things to share. How is this best done without diluting either one in the process?

The pressing issue brought the NUCS board of directors to appoint a committee in 1950 to study the admission of outside students. The concern clearly centered on admission of students from backgrounds other than those committed to the historic Presbyterian and Reformed creedal bases and, in a number of cases, with a lifestyle different from that evidenced by the people committed to that basis. The report, formally presented in 1954, reflected a growing receptiveness to opening the schools to children of all Christian parents, "although [these children] are not reared in the awareness of their covenant character."[6]

The committee drew a firm distinction between admitting students from evangelical, non-Calvinistic Christian homes and those from liberal or unchurched families. They would admit the former provided that "the parents are definitely informed of the Calvinistic character of the school ... [and] are plainly and courteously informed that only those committed to the creedal basis of the school may be members of the school society and hence have a voice in its affairs."[7]

Regarding "students from liberal Protestant, Catholic, Jewish, or non-church homes" the committee agreed with the concept that the ministers voiced in 1946, namely, that "admission of children

6. *Christian School Annual*, 1954, p. 81. Heerema, Aldrich Evenhouse, and John A. Van Bruggen were the committee members.
7. *Ibid.*

from such homes to Covenantal Christian schools, if allowed at all, should always be clearly seen as a concession on the grounds that the presence of such students ... [is] unjustified by our principles [and] involve[s] grave dangers to the virility and ultimately to the faith and spiritual safety of our Covenant children and youth."[8]

Although the delegates at the 1954 convention adopted the report as advisory policy, the issue did not rest there. In the next decade a great deal of thought and discussion centered on the question, For whom are Christian schools? Attitudes changes. The term *outsider* was almost completely expunged from the vocabulary. Promotional programs involving non-Calvinistic constituents and new admission policies were introduced, making Christian schools much more accessible to non-Reformed Christians.

While such changes were taking place on a theoretical and theological level, Christian schools with a modified structural format came into prominence on the community level. These were interdenominational schools. Later the term *community Christian school* came into vogue, especially in Canada, because this term was thought to be more definitive of the objective and the nature of such a school.

Such schools are listed (in Appendix B) for Glendale, San Diego, and Hayward, Calfornia; Sioux City, Iowa; Lansing, Michigan; and St. Petersburg. The Flint, Michigan, Christian school, when organized in 1952, had thirty-six denominations represented in its studentry. Between 1951 and 1963, a school in Flushing, New York, conducted classes in two churches, a Baptist and a Presbyterian church, a fact that reflected the school's interdenominational character. Most of these schools had few if any of the traditional NUCS constituents. Most were begun and supported by evangelicals who became increasingly aware of the differences between Christian and secular education. Recognizing their newness in the field and understandably wishing to be strengthened by a wider and more experienced fellowship, many initially joined the NUCS. Traditionally, where parents held the covenantal ideology, with its implications for education, education was nurture-oriented. The cutting edge was instruction for a deeper consciousness of the implications of God's sovereignty in all areas of life for a child who was

8. *Ibid.*, p. 82.

already considered one of God's people. The new variety of denominational backgrounds reflected more the idea that the school is a vehicle for child evangelism, although not to the exclusion of Christian nurture.

Generalizations are hazardous and sometimes profitless, but one candid observation must be made, namely, that this cooperative effort between Reformed and non-Reformed evangelicals was not totally successful. More experience in preparing for operating community Christian schools was needed.

A disheartening, dramatic example of one unsuccessful effort was the early cooperative experiment in Seattle.[9] In 1946, Fakkema initiated a school among families from Christian Reformed, Orthodox Presbyterian, Baptist, and other churches broadly defined as evangelical. Soon after the school opened, differences in theological assumptions and educational priorities became evident. Dispensationalists among the evangelicals assumed control and relationships deteriorated. The people who wanted to gain control resorted to courses of action that were not in accord with standard parliamentary procedure. Board members sometimes met without the president of the board, the Reverend Watson Groen first and later the Reverend Earl Setterholm. As differences increased, the Reformed contingent was not acknowledged at public meetings.

The result was a withdrawal of two groups and the formation of two other schools. Bellevue Christian School was organized by the Reverends Joseph and Albert E. Greene, Jr., and Setterholm, who, although new to the movement, were dedicated to the more traditional principles of Christian education. This was in 1950; they organized another school as a board-controlled school. This was to prevent the possible departure from acceptable objectives and programs by enthusiastic yet less informed pressure groups. The Greene brothers' parents, Mr. and Mrs. Albert E. Greene, Sr., donated a ten-acre site for the new school.

The Reformed contingent established a school in Seattle in 1952 with a firm guarding of Reformed and Presbyterian interests written into its constitution. After one year, the school was named

9. The source for this information is a tape prepared by Henry Vander Pol, Joseph Greene, and Jay Anema.

Watson Groen as a tribute to the minister who with kind determination led that group through the difficult early years.

The Seattle Christian School from which the two schools separated continued to operate and later to flourish. The animosity among the groups struggling for identity is no longer present. The three schools are now neighborly and, among other things, engage in interscholastic activities.

Another approach in seeking an answer to the question, For whom are Christian schools?, was through the mission-school concept that actually never got beyond the investigatory stage. Except for the Christian Reformed mission schools in Rehoboth and Zuni, New Mexico,[10] the Calvinist tradition has considered the mission school as atypical and somewhat outside its competence to evaluate as an institution of Christian nurture. However, the idea of using the Christian school as an agency in the work of home mission and church extension was seriously considered. While the Reverend Harold Dekker was minister of evangelism of the Back to God Hour in the early 1950s, he broached the subject with the NUCS and the home-missions board of the Christian Reformed Church. The NUCS, the Back to God Hour, and the Christian Reformed Church home-missions board jointly studied the feasibility of setting up such schools. All were well aware that a school of this kind would have to be subsidized. Salt Lake City, Utah, was selected as a pilot study. The home church was small and held promise for future growth. Representatives of the NUCS, John A. Vander Ark, the executive director, and Hemmo Schreuder, a board member from Denver, helped to establish a school in 1954. Christian Reformed churches in Denver graciously provided supplementary funds for three years, after which the school became self-supporting, although not without difficulty. This practice was encouraged in subsequent years, particularly by Harold Camping during his tenure as NUCS board member and president. Two factors, however, influenced the groups to abandon the practice. Complications arose in establishing Christian schools in commu-

10. For many years these schools used a child-evangelism strategy. According to the Reverend Peter Borgdorff, field secretary of the CRC Board of Home Missions, that policy was deliberately changed (c. 1970) in the Rehoboth and Crown Point schools. Children of former, evangelized students are now enrolled, and the orientation is toward Christian nurture. In Zuni, however, the evangelistic emphasis is still stronger than in other schools.

nities that were not ready and wholly supportive. In addition, already-established Christian schools increasingly needed funding from the churches in their communities.

Creedal Considerations

Making Christian education available to more families was one factor that gave rise to a major issue that was not without controversy, namely, the re-examination of the basis article of a school's constitution. One of the contributions of the Canadian wing of Calvinistic Christian schools was the discussion about the basis of Christian education and the formulation of an educational creed. Historically, the NUCS and its member schools have been identified with a particular ecclesiastical community in the Reformed tradition; that is, the Christian Reformed Church. This identity was reflected in the basis article of the constitutions or bylaws of local Christian schools: "The basis of the school is the Scriptures of the Old and New Testament, the infallible Word of God, as explicated in Reformed creedal standards."[11] This declaration was made to underscore not only a unified way of understanding the relationships of doctrine and life, but also to indicate that there are Reformed distinctives in education. However, at least three issues are raised by appealing to church creeds in a basis article. First, ecclesiastical creeds are a statement of faith, and although they contain implications for education, they do not sufficiently elaborate on principles by which educational policies may be developed. In this regard, it is further maintained, a church creed does not distinguish a school from a church or from other institutions expressive of the Christian faith. Second, resorting to church creeds decreases the necessity to examine what the Scriptures say about education. Finally, it is argued, ecclesiastical creeds

11. The NUCS model constitution. The basis article of the NUCS constitution read: "The basis of the National Union of Christian Schools is the Word of God as interpreted in the Reformed Standards. It is not an ecclesiastical body nor is it subject to any ecclesiastical organization. The government of the National Union of Christian Schools is autonomous being based upon the three-fold office of the believer — Prophet, Priest, and King.

"It is committed to the Reformed world and life view. Its educational principles must therefore by distinctively Reformed in emphasis and character."

This constitution was in effect from 1945 until 1972.

place unnecessary restrictions on membership in a Christian-school society and on its board of directors.

There had long been a desire to draw into Christian schools those who share ideals expressed in the Reformed faith as it applies to education, but who do not share all points of doctrine as expressed in Reformed creeds. In this context the motivation for forming an alternative to an ecclesiastical creed is to eliminate a possible needless offense to such people and by this same concern not ask them to jeopardize their integrity in signing such a doctrinal statement.

Others have also had a desire to establish interdenominational schools or, as the Dutch language has it, *algemeen Christelijke scholen* ("general" or "ecumenical Christian schools"). What some advocated was a general Christian statement of faith (*algemeen Christelijke geloof*) as a ground for cooperative action.

Perhaps one can understand better the drive for changing the historic position, the traditional requirements, by recalling some of the sensitive concerns in the Dutch immigrants' background. Having been molded in the Kuyperian tradition and having been caught recently in the crossfire of ecclesiastical battles in the Netherlands, the typical immigrant emphasized freedom from government and no church walls *(kerkelijke muren)*.

Many people, including teachers, were involved in the debates on this issue and many also were involved in the attempt to write an educational creed, a confessional statement expressive of the historical Christian faith as it relates to education. At the 1963 convention of the Canadian Christian Teachers Association, for example, R. Kooistra presented a draft of a creed and led a discussion on this issue. Actually the Ontario Alliance of Christian Schools (NUCS District 10) was the official body that sponsored the preparation of this draft. The issue was already envisioned when the alliance was formed in 1952. Ten years later, the Reverend Adam Persenaire, NUCS board member at that time, asked, on behalf of the alliance, that the NUCS board of directors "react" to the full text. The board hesitated to approve the text and asked for clarification of the meaning of the phrase *historic creeds of the Protestant Reformation* and what the implications were for membership in the Christian-school society and on the board as well as in classroom instruction.

The Association for the Advancement of Christian Scholarship

(AACS) sharpened the focus on this issue in its early years. The connection between the alliance's early interest in an educational creed and the association's formulation of one is obscure. No written record of the interaction seems to be available. However, in one of a series of articles about the history and significance of the AACS, Bert Witvoet, leaning on research done by C. C. Vanderiet, traced the development of the educational creed in that body.[12] At the October 17, 1956, meeting of the AACS board, Herman Dooyeweerd of the Free University in Amsterdam voiced his objection to the character of the doctrinal basis of the constitution and "advised that the society [AACS] should not bind itself to the confessions of the church, but only to the Scriptures." H. Evan Runner of Calvin College was asked to write a draft that would state "how an educational institution saw its task in relationship to the Scriptures." After a few years Runner's draft was given to a committee for refinement. Dirk H. T. Vollenhoven, also of the Free University, was asked to write the preamble. The educational creed as recast into its present format was adopted by the AACS in 1963.

While this creed was being prepared there were misgivings in other quarters. One who objected strongly was Peter Speelman, one of the organizers of the AACS and also an early participant in the Ontario Alliance. He says, "I was concerned about our view of the Bible. The Reformed confessions of church guard against heretical views of the Bible. If the Bible is to be the basis of our association, we need the confessions which tell us how to view the Bible."[13]

It would be unfair and unobjective to maintain that all who wanted to exclude the phrase *as explicated in Reformed creedal standards* wanted to be other than Reformed. These people hoped that an educational creed would bring out what Scripture teaches concerning education, be altogether in harmony with Reformed creedal statements, and give guidance in wrestling with the question, For whom are Christian schools?

The problem was not settled by 1965, despite repeated dealings with the matter on the district levels as well as by the NUCS board

12. *Calvinist Contact*, October 2, 1981, p. 8. The series recognized the association's twenty-fifth anniversary.

13. Reported in *Calvinist Contact*, October 2, 1981, p. 8.

and in convention proceedings. In fact, a revision of the NUCS bylaws and a model constitution for schools, which included an adaptation of its basis article, was not adopted by the NUCS House of Delegates until 1972. The new basis article, similar to the education creed developed in Canada, spelled out principles for Christian education, affirming convictions with respect to the Bible, creation, Jesus Christ, sin, schools, parents, teachers, pupils, community, and educational freedom. The NUCS basis article differs from the educational creed in that it retains the phrase *as explicated in Reformed creedal standards.*

Consolidations

A growth of enrollment coupled with the rapid growth of suburbs to which many Christian-school supporters were moving brought several communities to a new dilemma. Should a Christian school branch out with new schools that would become independent of the parent school? Or should there be centralization, organization, and control of schools within a well-defined area? For example, Holland, Michigan, Bellflower, California, and Edmonton added units to a growing system under one board of directors. Other areas such as Paterson, New Jersey, Grand Rapids, Michigan, and Chicago had long histories of having separate school societies and schools in different sections of the urban communities. A challenge of stewardship, however, pressed constituents to face these questions: Can Christian education be more efficient and effective by working in concert? If so, how should those goals be accomplished?

The Christian schools in the Paterson area were the bellwethers of consolidation. Involved were four elementary schools—North Fourth Street, Riverside, Midland Park, and Passaic (Pine Street)—and one high school, Eastern Academy.[14]

The year was 1948. A crisis loomed before the independent, local school societies. The accelerated enrollments were causing congestion in the schools. Building expansion or renovation was essential in every community. Eastern Academy had already

14. The information that follows was gleaned from a paper in the files of the Eastern Christian School Association, "History of Consolidation of the Eastern Christian Schools, 1948–1951."

launched a drive to obtain a new site and building. Satisfying the needs of all the schools threatened to require more than supporters could or would pay. Some leaders viewed consolidation as the viable solution.

The only existing body to conduct a study on the subject was the Eastern Alliance of Christian Schools (NUCS District 1), which appointed a committee of representatives from each school: Henry Piersma, Richard Hoekstra, John Kuipers, Milo Velsen, Ambrose Petzinger, Walter Hommes, Nicholas Hengeveld, John Last, Sr., Joseph Jellema, and Paul Heerema. Andrew Snoep, the Eastern representative on the NUCS board of directors, and Lambert Petzinger, who was well-qualified to plan and prepare "propaganda" — a good word in former days — were asked to join the committee.

The study identified aspects of consolidation that had not originally been seen as benefits: unification and integration of school policies and practices, including a unified curriculum.

The committee came up with eleven differing proposals for consolidation, the last of which found the best reception. It would retain three elementary schools to serve grades kindergarten through six; phase out Riverside as soon as possible; establish a junior high school, using the Eastern Academy building, for the entire area; erect a new senior high school; and organize a single board to operate all schools in the area.

In the three-year transition period the committee informed the people thoroughly through the printed page and forums. The school files show a chronological sequence of thirty-four meetings held in those formative years.

After two years of study, members of the five boards met to agree on details of a merger contract to be presented to the respective societies for ratification. All societies except Midland Park ratified the contract promptly. Midland Park rejected the merger contract because the society had funds in reserve for building a new elementary school in its area and was afraid that the consolidated board would use those funds to build the proposed high school in North Haledon. Midland Park's action was a big disappointment because it signaled a break in the cohesiveness of the Christian-school community. The other societies, however, proceeded with merger plans and on July 9, 1951, formed the Eastern Christian School Association. Within the month, Midland Park, having been assured that its funds would be kept for building in Midland Park, relented and by an overwhelming vote agreed to be included in the consolidation. The new association then cast a community-healing vote of 709 to 2 to accept the holdout society, thus laying to rest any overt dissension in the community.

At that meeting the board was authorized to engage an architect for the new senior high school, which was to be built on an attractive plot acquired from the Leonhard estate. The new board, under the competent leadership of John Hamersma, Jr., proceeded to operate the system with zeal and imagination. Among the strides it took was to set up the booster-club plan of financing Christian education. Every supporting church set up a club to raise money for the full cost of education for every school-age member of its church. The plan served as a model that many Christian-school communities emulate, with some modification, even to the present. The board also provided for an orderly building-expansion program. In 1959 a new elementary school was built in Wyckoff to meet the needs of a shifting population. This was one of the objectives of consolidation.

One objective was not realized immediately, namely, finding a superintendent to coordinate the administration of the new system. Having been unsuccessful in acquiring a person for the office, the board undertook a different strategy. The principals of the schools formed an administrative council and promoted active committees that were very much involved in administrative as well as policy-making decisions.

In Grand Rapids consolidation came later, although already in 1955 the Christian Education Society of the LaGrave Avenue Christian Reformed Church suggested the possibility by calling a meeting of all Christian-school boards and principals "to test sentiments for and against consolidation."[15] The initiative to follow up was laid at the door of an existing body known as the Grand Rapids Council of Christian Schools, embracing Baxter, Creston, Christian High, Mayfield, Oakdale, Seymour, Southwest, and West Side Christian schools. A precipitating step for action was the merger of the Baxter and Oakdale Christian schools in 1963. The shrinking enrollment at Baxter, owing to a changing neighbor-

15. Consolidation Study Report, 1964. Looseleaf file from the Grand Rapids Christian School Association office.

hood, the exodus of Protestant Reformed pupils to the newly-formed Adams Street Christian School, and temporary overcrowding at Oakdale led to the formation of United Christian Schools, a small-scale consolidation of two Christian schools.

In 1964 the Grand Rapids council, through a ponderous fourteen-person committee, undertook an extensive study that involved hundreds of people whose feelings toward consolidation ranged from adamant opposition to keen enthusiasm. Opposition stemmed generally from a deep sense of local loyalty, a "closeness to the scene" that embraced close parental contact, a fear of erosion of local interest and financial support, and fear of having a too-powerful central board of control. The Reverend Gordon Girod, a voice of the opposition, said the motivation for consolidation stemmed from the characteristic American assumption that bigness is better.

Like its New Jersey predecessor, the Grand Rapids study included provisions for uniform financial structures and even a consolidation of debts; building uses and projections about new facilities; the intraschool deployment of teachers; and the better coordination of curriculum and educational services. The Grand Rapids council's study committee stressed equalization of opportunity for children: "The only justification for any change from the existing pattern would be furnished by the hope that a new arrangement would provide a better level of education for all students of the community."[16]

The proposal to consolidate failed to win immediate support. The study committee and constituents agreed that unification was desirable, but they could not agree whether it should be accomplished via federation or full consolidation. The council dismissed the committee and appointed another, composed of fifteen persons, in 1966. Only three members were carried over: John Dykstra, Michael Ruiter, and Nicholas Wolterstorff. The unification effort went through another three years of wrestling and negotiating before a format was accepted. Philip Elve was appointed as the first superintendent of the one society, the Grand Rapids Christian Schools. There was one central board of trustees, but each school (called a district) retained an advisory committee and its own parent-teacher association. Subsequently two other groups in

16. *Ibid.*

Grand Rapids consolidated: the schools of the west side merged into an organization of their own, as did some schools of the southwest.

Institutional Obituaries

In a time when Christian education was prospering and many new schools were being established, one hardly thinks about the fact that some young schools expired before coming to maturity. An analogy might be made in writing about a family. If a member dies, that must be reported.

The facts of school closings are indicated in Appendix B. Reasons for their demise are not given, mainly because each situation is usually complex. The following schools apparently were victims of the shortage of teachers: Cleveland (East), Ohio; Monsey, New York; Dispatch, Kansas; Kirkwood, Pennsylvania; and Kenosha, Wisconsin. In every case, however, there were additional factors, one being the lack of a sizable enough supporting constituency.

Demographic problems (changing neighborhoods) brought about the closing of Englewood (Chicago), Baxter (Grand Rapids), and Century (Los Angeles). For Century, additional factors were that the state bought part of its property for the Harbor Freeway, its supporters were scattered in thirteen suburbs, enrollment was dropping, and interest was flagging.

In some instances, such as Comstock (Kalamazoo, Michigan), the enrollment was stagnant, with a projected decline; furthermore, the pupils could be accommodated in a nearby Christian school. Schools in Hawarden, Iowa; Riverton (Seattle); Tucson, Arizona; Canaan, Maine; Grangeville, Idaho; and Sun Valley, California, all were small. The financial base in every instance was narrow, qualified teachers were not readily available, leadership that led in establishing a school in some instances diminished in effectiveness, and the uphill struggle to maintain a school discouraged parents and members of the organization.

To read the obituaries of these and other schools naturally makes one sad. In a brighter and more grateful mood, one must realize that the casualities among Christian schools in this time frame, 1943–1965, were not nearly as numerous as those in a previous period. On balance one must bear in mind that it was the Christian instruction that went on in these buildings that really counted. The last president of one school, interviewed years later, readily responded with a strong yes when asked if, had he known the outcome, he would have done it all over again. "After all," he added, "we did what we knew was right at the time of opportunity and many are the lives that have been blessed and are still being blessed because of it." A most encouraging aspect of this issue is that Canadian Christian schools have almost no attrition. Every Christian school started since 1943 was still in operation in 1965.

Development of Christian High Schools

No segment of the Christian school systems grew as rapidly since 1943 as did the high schools. In 1943 there were only 12 bona fide high schools out of a total membership of 94 schools. By 1965 the total school membership was 277, of which 34 were high schools, 4 in Canada. The most dramatic increase was realized in the years since 1965. By 1980, there were 74 high schools out of 353 schools.

The development of Christian high schools reflects cultural changes as well as dedication to a cause. To understand better what has happened within the Christian system between 1943 and 1965, a flashback to happenings prior to 1943 is useful. When the NUCS was organized in 1920 there were six secondary schools: Chicago Christian High, Eastern Academy, Western Academy, Grand Rapids Christian High, Holland Christian High, and the now-defunct Grundy Academy. They were strongly oriented to college preparation and very definitely to teacher preparation. Christian-school boards fully expected, then and for many years afterward, to find teachers for their elementary schools in the graduating classes of high schools and academies. These graduates perhaps participated in a six-week summer session somewhere to be ready for the opening of school in September.

"In the 30's graduation from high school (or college even) was no longer the open sesame to employment and success it once had been."[17] There was a period when people, including proponents of Christian elementary schools, were indifferent to a high school education. They saw no need in it for making a living. For

17. V. T. Thayer, *Formative Ideas in American Education: From the Colonial Period to the Present* (New York and Toronto: Dodd, Mead, 1965), p. 310.

others, high-school education was a luxury unrelated to enriching life or entering various professions.

One of the strongest influences in accelerating the growth of Christian secondary schools was the rising educational level throughout Anglo-America, sheltered by stricter school-attendance laws. Before the 1950s many states and provinces did not require youth to be in school beyond the eighth grade or their sixteenth birthday. The memory of my years as a learning-many-things-fast principal of Western Christian High is replete with instances of meeting eighth-grade graduates and their parents and extolling the value of more formal education. My job was twofold: encouraging youth to attend high school and giving that experience a biblical rationale.

Structures of an educational system do reflect the times and the society that produced them. The academies became high schools, indicating a broader offering of courses, commensurate with the needs of more youth. Except for offering secretarial courses, the Christian high schools did not prepare students for specific jobs.

A significant influence, with both promotional and educational value, was the High School Principals' Conference of 1948. It was jointly sponsored by the NUCS and Calvin College. The agenda covered a wide range of issues on both theory and practice. Consideration was given to principles and the philosophy of Christian secondary education. Practical aspects of running a school were also discussed: management, public relations, curriculum, and particularly uniform standards. Frustrations, evidenced by questions dealing with how broad must the school's course offering be and what is distinctively Christian about many traditional courses, were apparent. The conference concluded with a mile-long list of services and curriculum projects that the principals requested of the NUCS and a strong desire to meet again next year.

Principals in attendance were Harvey Brasser and Henry J. Beversluis from Eastern Christian High; Fred Wezeman, Chicago; Cornelius Van Beek, Illiana; E. R. Post, Grand Rapids, Bert P. Bos and Ray Holwerda, Holland; Fred Westmaas, Northern Michigan; Fred Huizenga, Pella; John A. Vander Ark, Western Christian High, Hull, Iowa; Bernard Koops, Lynden, Washington; Oliver Buus, Bellflower; and Marius Van Vuren, Ripon, California.

A second jointly-sponsored conference was held in 1949. The

accent was on philosophy, an area in which many principals did not feel comfortable but learned from the professional philosophers, W. H. Jellema, Cornelius Jaarsma, and Henry Stob, and the men of Calvin's education department, Lambert Flokstra and J. L. De Beer. In addition to ones who attended the first conference, Gerrit De Vries (Kalamazoo), James Hoekenga (Grand Rapids), and Harold Tiemens (Bellflower) were present.

The conference became an annual event, broadening out in 1950 to include elementary principals. That year two groups were organized. In 1955, at the conference in Lynden, the secondary and elementary principals merged to form the ongoing organizaton called the Association of Christian School Administrators (ACSA). For several years thereafter, NUCS, Calvin College, and (after 1955) Dordt College subsidized the annual ACSA conference. Then for a period the NUCS administered a travel-equalization plan for principals in attendance. As the child (ACSA) grew, it became more and more independent of its parents, began to determine its own conference program, and after a few years, the principals' conference and NUCS convention programs were merged.

It became increasingly evident that Christian high schools were desired by many communities that allegedly could neither afford nor adequately populate a high school to the satisfaction of accrediting agencies. The concept of setting up district high schools took hold, especially in Canada. By 1965, four such schools were successfully launched in Canada: Hamilton (1957), Toronto (1963), and London (1965) in Ontario; and Frazer Valley (1964) in British Columbia. These mark the beginning of an extensive growth of Christian high schools in Canada, which by 1980 were twenty strong. There is an interesting commentary with respect to the development of Hamilton District Christian High. While it was in the formative stage, summer schools for public-high-school students were conducted under the auspices of the Ontario Alliance of Christian Schools. Courses taught by Jennie Visser and Persenaire included one titled "Approach to Christian Teaching." A future teachers college was discussed in visionary terms. A meeting of the Ontario Alliance advocated that the Christian high school in Hamilton might be a *voorloper* ("forerunner") of a Christian normal school. It was agreed, however, that full support ought to be given first to a good secondary school.

The need for Christian high schools steadily became a less debated issue. Their rationale lay to a great extent in an argument of analogy. Just as the public high schools in Anglo-America are cited as a means of preparing for an ideal society and promoting citizenship in democracy, so the Christian high school prepares for an ideal society, a different and richer one, a Christian community called the kingdom of God.

5

Relationships with Churches and Colleges

$\mathbf{H}$ad John Donne composed his immortal line with Christian education in mind he might have said, "No Christian school is an island." Interrelationships with the church, institutions of higher learning, and governments is no coincidence. The conviction that Christ is Lord in all areas of life provides the basic reason for fostering relationships between Christian day schools and such institutions, as well as the home.

Church-School Relations

The historical development of many Christian schools identified with the National Union of Christian Schools (NUCS) mirrors the long history of denominational emphases on the nurture of the church's children; a familiar term in the literature then and now is "covenant" children. One hardly needs to be reminded that the early Christian schools were church schools, brought into being and administered by the church. Leaders were firm in their belief that the well-being of the church depended in large part upon the maintenance of Christian schools.

This changed toward the end of the nineteenth century when immigrant teachers and ministers who had been influenced by Groen Van Prinsterer and Abraham Kuyper arrived from the Netherlands. They taught that each of the many spheres of life — family, state, church, society, commerce, education — has its own peculiar character and an internal structure subject to laws of its own determined by God.

Immigrant teacher-principal M. J. Veltkamp expressed the view that brought about the change in the 1890s: "There's too much the notion that 'the school is the handmaiden of the church.' " (Note the interesting Dutchism.)

Today the dominant view is that "the school is church-related, but it is not parochial.[1] It is organized not by churches, but by Christian parents who regard it as a natural outcome of their own commitment and as a continuation of the home."[2] Implications of this basic point of view have been amplified by many people in many forums. In a letter to the *New York Times* (Friday, December 8, 1961), the Reverend Daniel Hamilton summarized the role of the Christian school:

> The Christian school is the effort of Christian civilization to preserve itself. This movement is not to be construed as the crass employment of the school as an arm of the church's evangelical mission; rather, it is the question of the transmission of an integrated view of the whole of human life and destiny. . . .

We recognize that the Christian-school movement has developed its own genius and no longer belongs to or is administered by churches; nonetheless, a very close relationship exists between Christian schools and churches. One example would be the NUCS schools and the Christian Reformed churches in North America. Ministerial leadership, for example, is regularly sought and appreciated. George Stob employs figurative language to describe it: "Ministers are a supporting cast . . . chief propagandists because the voice that speaks with the weight and authority of the sacred office of the minister of the Word is greatly influential."[3]

The Christian Reformed Church (CRC) has from its beginning in 1857 been officially identified with Christian schools. It continued to promote the cause even after the organizations became

1. A parochial school, strictly speaking, is one owned by and under the supervision of a church.

2. Prospectus, Washington Christian School Society, Silver Springs, Maryland, 1960.

3. In his thesis, "The Christian Reformed Church and Her Schools," Princeton Theological Seminary, 1955.

separate. Synods of the Christian Reformed Church have made many official pronouncements, hortatory in nature, to help overcome obstacles to the growth of Christian schools and the alleged indifference of some parents and pastors. During this period the emphasis in official church bodies was broader than issuing hortatory statements. The synod of 1955, for example, commended to the churches "Principles of Christian Education," a document from a study committee. Also, in this period the churches, through participation in the NUCs teacher-recruitment program, helped to identify good prospects and provided grants-in-aid. As financial obligations of parents began to rise, many people began to fear that Christian education would be denied to some families. To counteract that possibility various plans that involved support from churches were initiated.

As the spokesman and the clearing-house for Christian schools, the NUCS helped churches in their efforts to promote Christian education. Besides preparing literature for easy distribution in churches, the NUCS continued the decade surveys, begun in 1930. The intent of the surveys was not only to collect data on the church affiliations of pupils attending Christian schools, but also to provide each church with statistics about the number and percentage of children who were attending Christian schools and stimulate greater patronage of the schools.

One of the most consequential happenings in church-school relationships stemmed from a resolution that delegates to the 1963 annual meeting adopted. The resolution asked for a "clarification of the relationships that ought to exist between churches and our Christian schools in financial matters."

A committee consisting of Lambertus Van Laar, Harry J. Bloem, Jr., E. R. Post, and Jacob De Jager prepared an eleven-page report that essentially called for churchwide support of all children in Christian schools. In developing its plan, the committee pointedly presented the scriptural and creedal bases for Christian schools, provided the history of official relationships between the church and school, and offered practical advice on relationships to the governing boards of both school and church.[4]

The suggested plan was labeled "Share the Cost." Although the

---

4. The report was published separately by the NUCS and also included in *Christian School Annual*, 1964, pp. 169– 180.

concept was neither new nor novel, it stressed the cooperative functioning of church and school. The report drew a ripple of adverse criticism from a few communities. Among these were Christian-school supporters in Edmonton, Alberta, who were very keen on their understanding of Kuyperian separate spheres of operation. The criticism served to caution against blurring the lines of authority and responsibility. With some variation, the plan continues to be used as a defensible implementation of a broader basis of support in communities.

Churches with theological similarities were involved in Christian day schools in this period, particularly the Reformed Church in America (RCA), the Protestant Reformed Church (PRC), the Orthodox Presbyterian Church (OPC), and the Canadian Reformed Church.

Although the Reformed Church in America did not officially endorse Christian day schools, the decade surveys of 1950 and 1960[5] revealed that 7.7 percent of the pupils in NUCS schools came from RCA homes.[6]

In 1960, 210 RCA churches were represented in Christian schools and from 1 to 134 pupils were from a single congregation. In almost all instances where a goodly number of RCA families had children enrolled in a Christian school, one or more board members were elected to represent that part of the school association.

The Orthodox Presbyterian Church, although handicapped in establishing schools by the relatively small size of its congregations, has always taken a vigorous stand in favor of Christian parental schools. Between 1936, the year of its second general assembly, and 1951, the date of its eighteenth general assembly,

---

5. Published in the *Christian School Annuals* of those years.

6. Interesting facets of this denomination's relationships to Christian education will be detailed in a subsequent publication. Dating back to 1628, the Dutch Reformed Church, the forerunner of the RCA, operated many Christian schools throughout the United States in the colonial period. This continued into the national period. By 1800, for example, in Pennsylvania alone, 124 of 188 churches operated parochial schools. But maintaining such schools became a losing battle during the nineteenth century. Many members believed then as they do now that the covenant doctrine does not necessarily imply sending children to Christian schools. Interest among some members, however, was sustained in the twentieth century. A phenomenon that bears more research and publicity is the fact that RCA families were wholly involved in establishing and maintaining Christian schools in certain areas, such as the prairie states.

the denomination registered twelve actions and recommendations concerning Christian schools. Each one challenged the membership to establish Christian schools. The Committee on Christian Education persistently brought recommendations to the general assemblies. Indicative of the church's theological stance, a subcommittee on covenant child training was appointed "to increase interest in Christian day schools, to provide better training of covenant children in the home ... and to promote interest in catechetical instruction in the churches."[7]

By 1945, the Committee on Christian Education presented the general assembly with "A Formulation of Specific Principles of Christian Education and Pedagogy. ..." This report not only provided a basis for the work of the committee but also gave a succinct rationale for the Christian day school. Several schools whose patrons are predominatly OPC have been formed, but in 1964 the committee still felt "the need to seek ways and means of confronting the constituency of the OPC with the need and opportunity in our day for Christian schools."[8]

The Protestant Reformed Church has a history of firm support for Christian education. There was both a clear sense of covenant obligation and a denominational identity with Christian day schools. Conviction was so ingrained in the members that the denomination has not felt the need to formally urge its members to use and support them. In its early years, from 1924 when the denomination was organized, until about 1950, members patronized existing Christian schools. An example of such patronage was the Baxter Street Christian School in Grand Rapids, Michigan, the school nearest the First Protestant Reformed Church. A proportionate number of board members were elected from the membership of the PRC, thus giving its members a voice in the control of the school. PRC teachers also served on the staff.

By 1950, however, denominational leaders became increasingly enamored of using the Christian school to bolster allegiance to the church. Some decried "common-grace schools," a not uncommon label for schools predominantly CRC. Adams Street Christian School, Grand Rapids, was then started, "dedicated to the prop-

7. Tenth general assembly proceedings, 1943, p. 36.
8. Cooperation between the general secretaries, Floyd Hamilton, Robert Nichols, and Roger Schmuur, and the NUCS has been evident.

osition that all academic subjects be taught from a PR perspective."[9] Such schools were, without exception, parental/and societal organizations. They were not parochial, although the tie between church and school in every instance was extremely close. Adams Street Christian School became a member of the NUCS in 1958 but, owing to internal denominational pressure, severed its relationship in 1960.

By 1965 there were five schools supported by the PRC. Today the denomination sponsors ten schools, nine elementary and one high school, which compose the Federation of Protestant Reformed Schools. The church and the federation continue a policy of noninvolvement with other Reformed schools. A unifying publication among them is *Perspectives in Covenant Education,* "published tri-annually ... by the Protestant Reformed Teachers' Institute."

Another Reformed body, the Netherlands Reformed Church, presents an interesting configuration among denominations that support Christian schools. A school of that church — the only one for many years — Hastings Street Christian School in Grand Rapids, dates back to 1908. In 1956, its site was lost to urban redevelopment, in this instance the cross-state freeway Interstate 96. The sponsoring congregation built a new school on Plymouth Road and thus kept the original school in operation under a new name.

This congregation controls the governing board. School-board elections are held at the annual congregational meeting and the consistory appoints three of its members to the school board. Interestingly, there is no denominational restriction for the teaching staff and pupils. Staff members are, of course, carefully screened. Teachers are asked to sign an agreement that outlines cardinal doctrines of the church. The future for Christian schools sponsored by the Netherlands Reformed Church bodes well. From the vantage point of the present, one can report that there is evidence of new zeal in starting Christian schools. Following the organization of one in Wyckoff, New Jersey, which joined the NUCS in 1975, seven other Netherlands Reformed schools have been formed in Canada and the United States.

Still another Reformed denomination must be acknowledged for its uniqueness in its theological position and commitment to

9. *Standard Bearer,* December 1, 1980, p. 235.

Christian schools with a corresponding viewpoint. Reference is made to the Canadian Reformed Church,[10] which since 1962 has developed a system of Christian schools. The John Calvin Christian School in Burlington, Ontario, was the first to be opened. At present there are seventeen in Canada and one in the United States. The latter is under the sponsorship of the only congregation of the denomination in the United States, the American Reformed Church in Dutton, Michigan. The Canadian Reformed Teachers College in Hamilton opened on September 8, 1981. It prepares teachers for the church's schools.

Two such schools, John Calvin Christian School in Burlington and the Coaldale (Alberta) Christian School, were members of the NUCS for a brief period, but chose to align themselves only with other schools sponsored by their denomination. The teachers' college has taken the same stance.

After presenting the relationships of the foregoing Reformed churches to Christian schools and telling some significant developments that do not conform to a rigid time frame, one must not neglect to include the Reformed Presbyterian Church, Evangelical Synod (RPCES). Covenant College at Lookout Mountain, Tennessee, is its college.

The Reformed Presbyterian Church in North America — identified in Christian educational circles by its college, Geneva College at Beaver Falls, Pennsylvania — has not been basically committed to supporting Christian day schools. However, Johannes Vos, a long-time instructor there, will be remembered for his brilliant and valiant defense of Christian education as a covenant obligation.

Further commentary on other Reformed or Presbyterian churches that now have a significant relationship with Christian schools, such as the relatively new Presbyterian Church in America (PCA), properly belongs to a later era.

Retracing the history of church and school relationships would be incomplete without a reference to a most effective outreach

10. The leader and founder of this denomination was the Dutch scholar and theologian, Klaas Schilder, whose views on the covenant and article 31 of the church order were judged to be incompatible with the official position of the mother church, the Gereformeerde Kerken in Nederland (GKN). This development occurred in the Netherlands in 1944 and was evidenced among the postwar immigrants from the Netherlands and the institutions they established.

of the Christian Reformed Church, namely, the Back to God Hour. Through the preaching of its spirited ministers, the Reverend Peter Eldersveld (now deceased) and Joel Nederhood, and also several guest ministers in bygone years, the apologetic for Christian schools was and still is dynamically presented. The sermons and other addresses of the Back to God Hour personnel constitute a literary and theological heritage par excellence.

Thus, while nearly all NUCS member schools are free from direct church control, they are, nonetheless, strongly church-related. The Christian Reformed Church unquestionably is the denomination predominantly identified with promoting and supporting Christian schools. The trend, however, has been toward participation of more Calvinistic churches and also more members of non-Reformed churches who appreciate the Reformed emphasis in education. Decade surveys reporting on denominational representation in NUCS schools indicated a gradual percentage increase in the number of such pupils as well as greater interaction between schools and student-supplying churches, an encouraging trend.

Relationships with Colleges

As this period of Christian-school history began, there was also the beginning of a new interest on the part of Christian-school patrons for cooperating with and demanding cooperation from Calvin College, the main source of trained teachers. At the same time constituents generally were open-minded and inquisitive about the desirability of establishing junior colleges that could promote better teacher education. This cooperative spirit had not always been present. True, there had long been a vital concern regarding the professional training and status of Christian-school teachers, but how to achieve the goals remained an ongoing issue. It was generally agreed that too many teachers in early Christian schools were poorly equipped.

While the case for college education and professional training was argued, there was no common mind on the specifics of teacher education. Many leaders in Christian elementary and secondary schools carried on, harboring a grudge against leaders in higher education over both the content and the control of teacher education. The original constitution (1920) of the NUCS called for "establishing and maintaining ... a Christian normal school or ... giving moral support to existing institutions which give reasonable guarantees of furnishing our schools with thoroughly equipped teachers."[11]

The struggle over both establishing and controlling teacher education belongs to a period just prior to the period of our concern in this book. However, to understand better the situation in the mid-1940s, a quick flashback of some basic developments may well be given.

An experiment in conducting a society-sponsored Christian normal school was begun in 1919 in the Franklin Street Christian School in Grand Rapids, but survived only two years because it drew so few students and was strapped financially. The earliest Christian secondary schools, particularly Grundy Academy (1916), Chicago Christian High (1918), and Western Academy (1919), were organized with teacher education as one purpose for being established. There was a time, in fact, when these schools, having been formally charged (or tactfully assumed) by their organizers to be the training ground for teachers of Christian schools, asked the NUCS for moral and, if possible, financial support for their education programs.

Calvin College

Calvin College was officially born in 1894 when nontheological students were admitted to the literary department of the seminary. The curriculum, although virtually what was taught in academies, contained some teacher-education courses. It is not generally understood that the chief motivation for establishing (reorganizing) Calvin College was to prepare teachers for Christian schools.[12] In 1920 Calvin became a full-fledged, four-year college and gradually added more teacher-training courses. Some vocal Christian-school leaders continued to be dissatisfied with the slow implementation of what to them should have been good teacher preparation. They were also unhappy with the evident inconsistency that the parents controlled the elementary and secondary schools while the church (CRC) controlled the college.

11. This language appears in article 4 of the bylaws. This was to help the NUCS to achieve one of its purposes as set forth in the constitution, article 4.
12. Acts of Synod, 1922.

Recognizing the problem, the Reverend J. J. Hiemenga, the first
president of the college, attempted to bring a truce to the factions
through cooperation rather than through independent courses of
action. With a stroke of diplomacy, he brought about the establishment of an education department at Calvin College in 1923,
which was precisely what the NUCS desired. The NUCS board
responded to the development by granting a six-hundred-dollar
stipened to a person of its choice, Henry Van Zyl, a Christian-
school teacher and principal, to prepare for teaching in the new
department.

On the surface the issue of sponsorship was quiescent. The
education department expanded its curriculum and staff, soon to
include Johannes Broene, Lambert Flokstra, and Anne Holkeboer.
During this period a remote form of cooperative action between
marginally qualified teachers and Calvin College was conducted
through correspondence courses. A joint committee consisting of
then-President Broene and Dean Albertus Rooks of Calvin College, along with Mark Fakkema and Dorr Kuizema, representing
the NUCS, worked out a series of correspondence courses for
teachers who did not have proper credentials. But that was not
the end of insistence by principals especially on more direct Christian-school involvement in teacher training. Needled by a few alliances, especially the Chicago and Western alliances, the NUCS
raised the issue of sponsorship again in 1927. Its educational committee proposed three plans: first, giving moral support to the
normal (teacher-training) work that was given in existing colleges;
second, establishing a centrally located Union Normal College,
independent of Christian colleges then offering normal courses;
and third, asking one of our Christian colleges to entrust its normal department to the care of the union.

It appeared that the committee that proposed the alternatives
favored the third option. The board of directors, however, chose
a less precipitous course and set up an advisory committee composed of Henry Hekman, Garrett Heyns, and Richard Postma. Following the path of cool deliberation, the committee reported that
"important improvements have been made during the last couple
of years at Calvin and we are pleased to learn that further improvements are being contemplated."[13] The committee, too, was

13. Minutes, NUCS board of directors meeting, June, 1929.

"impressed by ... the practical phase of the normal work," heartily endorsed the work carried on at Calvin College, and advised the board to adopt the first plan. The board concurred and further decided "to give publicity to the findings of the committee."

In the 1940s a new impulse was felt for cooperation between the constituents of Christian education and the institution that prepared most of the teachers. What accounted for renewed motivation was the NUCS's shift in emphasizing the educational rather than the promotional aspect of Christian education.

The NUCS board of directors in 1947 took the initiative to set up a committee for cooperation between Calvin College and the NUCS. Although there was a desire on the part of some to counter the liberal-arts exclusiveness, which Christian-school teachers felt permeated the college board and faculty, there was a move to enlist the goodwill and cooperation of the college in a wide range of mutual concurrences about Christian education. The enabling leadership of Jacob Van't Hof was evident. Not to be underestimated was the professionally effective manner in which William Spoelhof, president of Calvin College, responded to the request for a committee for cooperation.

The enormous aspiration, made into a committee mandate, had many aspects: one was to help unify elementary and secondary schools and another was to make the transition from high schools to college more viable for college-bound students. A committee of top-ranking college faculty members and representatives of the NUCS was operational in 1947–1948.

The committee's agenda consisted of studies on the philosophy of Christian education and the place of philosophy in the teacher-education program; ways and means of recruiting promising students for teaching positions; certification; uniform credits for Christian high schools; consideration of additional courses in school administration; more intensive directed-teaching programs; the degree of emphasis of art, language, practical arts, and related matter in the Christian-school curriculum; and, added to the ponderous list, a discussion of the junior-college movement.

Similar cooperative efforts continued to have a strong influence on major aspects of teacher education. In 1950 the NUCS took a stand that a minimum of a four-year college education should be the goal for the training of all Christian teachers and encouraged all schools to abide by minimum requirements set by the respective state boards of education or ministers of education. Knowing that Calvin College was de-emphasizing the two-year teacher-education program, the NUCS (through the committee on cooperation) submitted a plan to give tentatively to the two-year students the twelve-week directed-teaching course that the four-year students received. The two-year course, however, was phased out soon after the resolution was adopted, because teacher education increasingly became equated with a baccalaureate degree.

In the early 1950s there was a slight tiff within the committee over the question of Calvin's sponsorship of summer extension courses in northwest Iowa and southern California. The college felt it could not do so, owing largely to inability to provide a satisfactory library and a teaching staff. The rationale seemed tenuous to the NUCS representatives, but Calvin offered a significant reduction in summer-school tuition as an inducement to get teachers to come to the campus. Plans to operate off-campus summer courses did not materialize until after 1965, when Ontario, Canada (NUCS District 10), entered its plea.

The NUCS's concern for qualified teachers was highlighted again in 1962 when, in a resolution submitted to the annual convention, the board of directors said, "There is evidence that certain schools are engaging substandard qualified [teachers] by choice." A rough paraphrase of this is that a few boards found substandard teachers easier on the school budget; their salaries were cheaper. This stimulated cooperative effort among controlling groups in popularizing summer-school sessions.

One of the outstanding services of the committee was to sponsor principals' workshops and the annual conferences that were also underwritten by Calvin College and the NUCS. This resulted in the formation of the Association of Christian School Administrators (ACSA).

Although it is difficult to measure or determine the effectiveness of the cooperative venture, it is valid to conclude that the committee influenced significantly the development in several aspects of teacher education. Among the other things, courses in earth science were introduced, and courses about the Bible, art, and other subjects explicitly beneficial to teachers were expanded. These courses eventually led to the granting of advanced degrees by collegiate institutions.

The committee for cooperation continued as a vital link between Christian schools and collegiate-level work until 1971. Its agenda became more formalized, and its role became that of supervising jointly-sponsored conferences and scholarship programs. As the NUCS staff grew, the NUCS director and the administrator of the School Relations Department, Ivan Zylstra, performed the duties assigned to the committee. After fourteen years the committee, with a commendable service record, was phased out.

The Junior-College Movement

The junior-college movement evoked the attention of the Christian Reformed denomination in the late 1940s. There were many roots to this matter, as there are in every instance of a healthy growing plant. For one thing, deeply imbedded in the Presbyterian and Reformed tradition is an encouragement of serious study and learning opportunities on every level — grade school, high school, junior college, (senior) college, university, seminary — the level is of little importance. The lordship of Christ on every level was and is the important thing.

Second, with a growing population, a growing level of prosperity, and a growing awareness of the wider range of opportunities that higher education can provide, it took no great wisdom to predict a growing support nationwide — also among Christians — of college education.

Finally, it should be mentioned that local or regional control of both ecclesiastical and educational institutions has long been a part of the heritage of Christian-school supporters.

A study committee that reported to the synod of 1948 commented favorably on developing Christian junior colleges. Another committee was appointed and reported to the synod of 1950 that it did not feel the constituency was ready for regional junior colleges.[14]

Synod adopted the latter committee's report and disseminated widely a digest of it. The committee allowed that "the demand for junior colleges among our Christian Reformed people is regional, arising primarily from those areas where there is an acute Christian school teacher shortage. It is especially vocal in Northwest

14. Members of the committee were Herman Kuiper, Lambert Bere, Bert P. Bos, Peter A. Hoekstra, William Spoelhof, Samuel Steen, and Ralph Bronkema.

Iowa and the Bellflower area of California."[15] Also reported was that there was "no pressing insistence" for a junior college in the Paterson, New Jersey, area, "no substantial demand" in the Pacific Northwest, and "no lively interest" in the Chicago area.

The study committee disclosed a fact that it discovered from the survey it had made: "Wherever the demand [for a junior college] occurs it is a demand arising from the educated leaders in these areas and from those who sense the value of higher education for their children. The survey does not indicate that the demand arises from the grass roots of the denomination."[16]

The committee gave a terse summary on lessons to be learned from past experiments — Grundy College and the Chicago Christian Junior College. "In the case of Grundy," the report states, "there were primarily two factors which led to its failure. The first of these was a lack of authoritative supervision and the second was the Depression. Lessons to be derived from the Chicago ... experiment ... include the fact that the teaching staff was not all a like-minded group, with a common view of life and education; [the college lacked] a building of its own ...; owing to the Depression, money was hard to get."[17]

The report aptly called attention, without prejudice or resolution, to other factors: the cost; the challenge of accreditation, adequate facilities, and qualified teachers; and the thorny issue of church versus society control. The committee, appropriately no doubt, urged strong cooperation with Calvin College and stimulated the already-opened task of making "clear for our day the meaning and task of the Kingdom of God"[18] (presumably as it had a bearing on the junior-college movement).

Dordt College

Without a doubt 1955 was a year of a major contribution to teacher education and a tribute to cooperative workings of Chris-

15. From the digest of the committee's report, published by the 1950 synod, p. 4.

16. *Ibid.*, p. 8.

17. *Ibid.*, p. 8. (The phrase *lack of authoritative supervision* refers to the fact that some aid for Grundy came from non-Reformed groups; detractors charged that this resulted in compromise. Also, the basis of agreement between Grundy and Calvin College was too hasty. Therefore, misunderstandings surfaced and caused discontent.)

18. *Ibid.*, p. 12.

tian elementary, secondary, and higher education. It was the year Dordt College was established.

Classis Ostfriesland (now called North Central) in Iowa initiated the movement of establishing a Christian junior college in the Midwest when it sent a communication to the then-existing fellow CRC classes Minnesota, Orange City, Pella, and Sioux Center in 1937. A joint committee of the five Midwest classes was set up, and at its first meeting in Kanawha, Iowa, the committee concluded that a junior college was desirable for the ostensible reason of getting more local youth into a Christian college. The committee met with representatives of Calvin College board of trustees and obtained a favorable hearing. This early momentum, however, came to an abrupt halt with the outbreak of World War II in 1941. Before the war ended, the Christian schools in the area became restive over the dearth of qualified teachers. In 1944 the Western Christian School Alliance (later known as NUCS District 6) took up the problem, repeated that the need for a junior college was urgent, and appointed a committee to investigate the possibility of establishing an accredited summer school in conjunction with Calvin College. The alliance also urged the classes to revive their initial action.

Progress was further delayed by waiting for the 1948 and 1950 synods of the CRC to respond about the advisability of having junior colleges in various areas of the denominational concentration. Synod bandied the issue around and failed to come out with a clear directive, although it did acknowledge there was a need for junior colleges. Then, in a manner too common in equivocating assembly reports, it guessed that the constituency of the Christian Reformed Church was not ready for junior colleges. Summer schools did not result, partly because, as stated earlier, Calvin resisted and partly because the issue of ecclesiastical versus society control was not resolved.

The alliance proceeded deliberately to get a college underway, mainly to ease the shortage of qualified teachers. In 1953 it sponsored two mass meetings in Rock Valley and Hull, Iowa, during which the Midwest Christian Junior College Society was organized, a constitution adopted, Sioux Center selected as the site, and building plans authorized. The attempt to get started in 1954 was scrubbed, owing to the locale's inability to finance a building in such a short time.

Midwest Christian Junior College dedicated its first building on
September 1, 1955, and got underway with thirty-five students and
five professors: the Reverend Cornelius Van Schouwen, Leonard R.
Haan, Nick Van Til, Douglas Ribbens, and Peter Van Beek. Administrative duties were to be handled by the whole faculty.

By 1956 the society adopted a new name for the college, namely,
Dordt College. This was a testimony and a verbal acknowledgment
of its Reformed heritage. (For a short time the modern spelling
Dort was entertained, but the original rendering prevailed.)

One cannot rightly claim that Dordt College was established
exclusively for the purpose of educating teachers for Christian
schools, but that had high priority. By 1958 Dordt enrolled 139
students, 78 of whom were in teacher training. The Reverend B. J.
Haan, in the capacity of president of the board of trustees, put the
issue in perspective when he spoke on "persistent forces which
confront us" in 1957. "Undeniable is the continued increase in
teacher shortage complicated by ever growing demands for better
qualified teachers."[19] He amplified the point by referring to the
demand of the states for certified teachers, a better-educated community to satisfy, and the need for Christian scholarship in applying Calvinistic principles.

Haan was appointed president in 1959, a position he held with
distinction until his retirement in the early 1980s. Throughout
these years Dordt and Calvin colleges shared the obligation and
the privilege of preparing most of the teachers who would be
serving in NUCS-affiliated Christian schools.

Trinity Christian College

Christian college education in Chicago or, more accurately Chicagoland, as the larger Chicago area is affectionately called, pre-
dates this period. I refer to the short-lived experiment of the
Chicago Christian Junior College in the 1930s. During Fred Wezeman's time as principal of Chicago Christian High, an extension
of the high school was effected and college-level classes were
held here. One objective of the founding group, evidently, was to
provide a Christian educational witness to high-school graduates
in the community. Participation was not restricted to graduates
of Chicago Christian High. The relatively short duration

19. Editorial, *Dordt College Voice*, January, 1957, p. 1.

(1933 – 1936) is attributed to bad economic times that contributed to a failure to acquire a satisfactory enrollment and a building of its own. Unfortunately there was also a rankling suspicion among potential patrons that the theological and educational footings were not sound.

One episode illustrates that point. One evening while college classes were being conducted there was also a public meeting held in the building. An attending patron rapped on the classroom door of Gerrit De Vries, who taught in both schools, and asked who was teaching in the adjacent classroom. The instructor was Ralph Jansen, who had been under severe criticism, charged with liberal theological views, and deposed from his position at Calvin Seminary. The inquirer doubtless was eager to pin suspicion on the college and Wezeman. Although no formal action against the college was reported, this vignette is indicative of the tension that prevailed.

In 1950, the Christian Reformed synodical study committee on junior colleges reported that, based on a survey made, "at the present time no lively interest in a junior college is arising from the people in the Chicago area. The majority of those interested favor an institution of a community college type."[20]

By 1952, interest in establishing a local Christian college seemed suddenly to come to a new expression. The prime movers, according to Derke Bergsma, who was involved with Trinity Christian College at an early stage and continued to be until 1982, were not the leaders in the area of Christian schools. A group of community leaders, from many walks of life and interested in Christian education at all levels, provided the impetus for the new movement. By that token, one can understand that the preparation of teachers for Christian schools was not as much of a motivation for founding the college as was the case at Dordt College.

The degree to which Christian-school leaders were involved at the outset may be nonetheless a bit moot. Discussions for the issue were conducted in two Christian-school forums: the Chicago Principals' ("P") Club and NUCS District 3. Also, the fact that Christian-school spokesmen, one of whom was Richard Prince (who served as the first administrative officer), were wholly in-

20. Reported in Acts of Synod, 1950.

volved in the founding of the institution indicates strong interaction with the existing Christian-school movement.

Trinity Christian College Association was organized in 1956. A golf course in Palos Heights, Illinois, was purchased in 1959 to serve as its campus. The clubhouse and pro shop were remodeled; the college opened for classes that fall with six fulltime and five parttime faculty members. The fulltime teachers were Prince, Gerda Bos, David Holwerda, Jack Musch, Calvin Seerveld, and Robert Vander Vennen, who also served for a time as administrative head.

The history of Trinity's development and relationship within the Christian-school movement belongs in a more recent period, the years since 1965. Thus, only a brief reference to Trinity is made here. In 1966 Trinity Christian College was developed into a four-year, degree-granting liberal-arts college and Alexander De Jong was inaugurated as the first president. In quick succession Gordon Werkema and Dennis Hoekstra served as presidents, followed by Gerard Van Groningen, the incumbent president.

Significant in this historical account is that in the early 1980s the college introduced a teacher-education program with certifi-

cation in business education, home economics, and industrial arts, thus providing needed services not offered by other Christian colleges in the NUCS fraternity.

Reformed Bible College

Under the earlier name *Reformed Bible Institute* (RBI), the college dates back to 1939, when it began holding classes in an upper storefront flat on Wealthy Street in Grand Rapids. The first instructor was Johanna Timmer, who sixteen years later became the first teacher-principal of Philadelphia-Montgomery Christian High School. Actually, however, the beginnings of the college must be attributed to the spearheading work of Fakkema, assisted by laymen friends in Chicago, George Van Heyningen and George J. Stob. Classes were held in Roseland before steps were taken to organize a Bible school in Grand Rapids. Among the founders of the Grand Rapids school were the Reverends H. J. Kuiper and John Schaal. According to the Reverend Schaal, who also had a long tenure as a teacher there, RBI was established at a time when thirty to forty other Bible schools were being formed, a phenomenon in the history of American Protestantism for which no ready explanation has been made.

The ministry of the college was and is to train students for evangelistic and educational service through church and mission. From the humble beginning, Reformed Bible College (RBC; the name was changed in 1971) expanded its program under the offices of its two presidents, the Reverends Dick Walters and Dick Van Halsema. It now offers two associate degrees and a baccalaureate degree in religious education. Although the college does not presume to provide teachers for Christian schools and is not accredited for that purpose, it is accredited by the American Association of Bible Colleges and approved by the Michigan Department of Education. As of 1981, RBC was given state authorization to grant a master's degree in religious education. Several teachers in Christian day schools studied for a time at RBC.

As the college expanded, it engaged some nonministerial teachers, particularly instructors with experience in Christian elementary and secondary schools. Among the early ones was Katie Gunnink. Other employees, such as Jack Stoepker, who had served as business manager at NUCS and had participated in the Christian School Pension Trust Fund, came aboard. The basic requirement for participation was that the employing agency must be a member of the NUCS. In that context the RBC in 1964 became an affiliate of the NUCS, which obligingly set up a membership category called affiliate membership. The NUCS did not, and Christian Schools International (CSI) does not now, presume to serve affiliate members in the same manner in which it serves elementary and secondary schools. The benefits of affiliate membership in time grew to be greater than mere qualification for the financial-security measures, the pension plan, and group health insurance, however significant these are. Fundamental to the affiliate membership are moral support in a common cause and camaraderie with fellow professionals.

From the precedent of the RBC's affiliate membership, a sizable network of Christian liberal-arts colleges with education departments have subsequently become affiliate members. Several Christian schools for special education also maintain an affiliate membership with CSI. In 1965 there were four affiliate members. By 1981 the number had increased to twenty-five.

Covenant College

Covenant College came into being in Pasadena, California, in 1955 under the auspices of the Evangelical Presbyterian Church, which in 1965 merged with the Reformed Presbyterian Church to become the Reformed Presbyterian Church, Evangelical Synod. Robert Rayburn was president of the college, and a student body of twenty-three (not all fulltime) students convened.

In 1956, the college began an eight-year residence halfway across the country, in St. Louis, Missouri, with an enrollment of sixty students. The college shared facilities with Covenant Theological Seminary, which began its first year that fall. To provide room for an expanding enrollment, the board of trustees shortly thereafter, in 1961, accepted a twenty-room mansion as a gift and had it moved to the new campus.

The college soon outgrew this shared facility and at the end of nine years prepared to make another move. A group of Southern businessmen, spearheaded by Harold Finch and Hugh Smith, proposed to buy a luxury hotel on Lookout Mountain, Tennessee. This meant an arduous task of converting the hotel to a college and moving a staff of twenty-five with families, plus necessary equipment.

The "settling in" went smoothly. Under the leadership of Marion Barnes, who became president in 1965, and successive deans John W. Sanderson and William S. Barker, the college developed a highly qualified faculty and excellent curriculum that led to full accreditation in 1971. It became an affiliate of NUCS in 1969.

According to Registrar Rudolph Schmidt, the college's vision to prepare teachers for Christian schools was made a reality through the engagement of teachers such as Geraldine Steensma, who was the first director of teacher education, and Nelle Vander Ark, who in addition to teaching was commissioned to promote Christian education in the denomination. Covenant College became a dynamic force in promoting Christian education among the RPCES membership and in preparing teachers for Christian schools. In 1982 the RPCES joined with the Presbyterian Church in America, which is now the college's sponsoring denomination.

Institute for Christian Studies

One other category of affiliate membership, however, ought to be mentioned and illustrated at this time. The category is Christian study centers or institutes. The Institute for Christian Studies, in Toronto, was organized in 1967. Its parent organization, the Association for the Advancement of Christian Scholarship (AACS), was begun in 1956 with the avowed long-range goal of developing a Christian university.[21] The AACS became an affiliate member of NUCS in 1968. Hendrik Hart, John Olthuis, and Bernard Zylstra were the staff members. Although the parent organization and the Institute have Calvinistic higher education as their principal concern, they cherished interaction with the NUCS and its elementary and secondary schools. The Institute, like other affiliate members, is witness to the conviction that Christian faith and life are to be integrated at all stages and levels of maturity.

The CSI system of schools is enriched by past and ongoing relationships with Christian institutions of higher education.

21. Bert Witvoet's informative review (with commentary) of the history of AACS appears in several issues of *Calvinist Contact*, fall, 1981.

6

Relationships
with Government

The relationship of Christian schools to the wide range of government agencies is a many-faceted subject. For that reason, to write the history of this issue with something more profitable than euphonious generalizations is difficult. Fortunately, there are two ingredients about which there can be no sidestepping: ideologies and people.

A significant document for Reformed thinking about relationships with government is one of the church creeds, the Belgic Confession, specifically article 36. The task of government is to administer justice. That means, among other things, punishing the evildoer and protecting those who do well (Rom. 13). Chapter 23 of the Westminster Confession speaks in a similar vein.

Christian-school constituents have at times found it difficult to articulate their desire for implementation of justice. Although Anglo-America theoretically is committed to maintaining a pluralistic society, yet the dominance of a civil religion propagated in the public schools seems pervasive.

To live a life consistent with one's faith is, of course, a basic freedom. The critical point is whether the rights of minority groups, such as Christian-school patrons, will be honored. In the *Calvinist Contact* the Reverend Arie Van Eek pinpointed the issue when he wrote, "Individual rights are meaningless unless their rights in concert with other like-minded people are honored."[1] The right to

1. February 2, 1981. Van Eek is executive secretary of the Council for Christian Reformed Churches in Canada.

exist is one thing, but is not enough to give substance to the ideal of justice for all. Each bona fide school has a civil right to expect application of justice in rules that pertain to the operation of schools. Fellow citizens who think in terms of a civil religion, however, too often do not understand that this right applies to Christian schools.

Three facets must be considered to understand the issues more adequately. First is an account of the struggle between parental associations and the state for the control of the education of children. Second is the unfinished story of financial aid to Christian schools. Third is a synopsis of significant United States Supreme Court decisions in this period (refer to Appendix C).

Christian-school advocates have long been targets of cheap criticisms and misleading innuendos that suggest they are not in the mainstream of the Anglo-American body politic. Christian schools are sometimes described as ostrich-headed; safe places to grow up away from bad wolves; and out of touch with culture and politics.

If such criticisms have a degree of truth, which is dubious, may they tend to keep us humble even though they do not portray the situation accurately. There were tensions in this period between advocates of public and private schools.[2] Actually, there have always been tensions on this subject. In the 1920s, for example, the state of Michigan attempted to close all parochial and Christian schools. The attempt failed because Protestants and Roman Catholics who favored private schools closed ranks on a common cause and aggressively fought it. Fears were intensified in the 1930s when Robert M. Hutchins, president of the University of Chicago, proposed a "planned society" in which students would early be guided into vocational choices. Christian schools, he averred, were not capable of offering the needed curricula for that purpose.

---

2. In conjunction with the debate about public support, the terms *private*, *nonpublic*, and *independent* are often used interchangeably and sometimes instead of the term *Christian*. The word *nonpublic* is less desirable for several reasons, primarily because it is negative and also because it does injustice to the public-service character of Christian education. The term *independent*, oddly, does not have the same meaning in Canada as in the United States. In the United States it is used to denote private, nonreligious schools, whereas in Canada it refers to all private schools.

Such happenings seem to suggest that Christian schools were still in a state of cultural isolation and were not enjoying good relations with governmental units and the public generally. Evidence for this presupposition, however, is lacking. In the United States, government regulations in many aspects of society, including education, were minimal in the 1940s. In most states, Christian schools followed requirements to be open a specified number of days per year; to submit attendance records; to be subject to fire, health, and safety ordinances; to teach basic subjects prescribed possibly by the state legislature; and in some instances, to test student performance on state-prepared or nationwide objective tests.

There are in the history of Canada and the United States glaring examples of discrimination against private, nonprofit schools in the area of taxation of property. Two examples will be cited here, one in California and one in Ontario.

California for many years had the dubious distinction of being the only state that taxed the property of non-tax-supported elementary and secondary schools. (Colleges were exempt.) In 1951, the California state legislature granted tax exemption to such schools and Governor Earl Warren signed the bill into law.

Opposition to the provision soon began to mount and a referendum was placed on the next ballot. California voters sustained the state legislature at the polls in 1952 by an exceedingly close vote. That was not the end of the matter. Opponents renewed their assault on the newly established freedom from taxation by throwing the issue into court, arguing basically that tax relief is in effect a subsidy to "religion." Litigation was carried all the way to the United States Supreme Court and opponents to tax exemption lost that final battle.

This movement to handicap nonpublic schools continued with intensity. The next attack by the opponents was to propose an initiative in the form of a constitutional amendment. The proposal was so drastic that everybody concerned with religious institutions of all kinds got behind the movement to stop such action. One very effective organization to counter the move was Protestants United Against Taxing Schools. James Zoetewey, a Christian-school leader in Bellflower and a member of the National Union of Christian Schools board of directors, was the treasurer. The initiative was soundly defeated at the polls in 1958 and the historic constitutional principle of nonprofit schools having their property tax-exempt was preserved in California.

The situation in Ontario was and is vastly different. As recently as the 1970s, a provincial tax-reform package that included the proposal to tax Christian school property was launched. Many individual Christian schools as well as the Ontario Alliance of Christian Schools (NUCS District 10) strongly protested the proposal.[3]

To cite more evidence that there was much concern over government-school relationships, a look at the selection and treatment of several related NUCS convention themes (1926, 1943, 1952, 1962, and 1964) is revealing.

The thesis running through virtually every speech and paper at the 1926 convention was that "the best Christian is the best citizen," a paraphrase of Daniel Webster's famous line that what makes a person a good Christian makes him a good citizen. It was reminiscent of the words from Scripture, "Righteousness exalts a nation," and from William Gladstone, who said, "Try to make good conscientious Christians out of your children and Great Britain will be satisfied with them as citizens." Speakers observed that the "odium of foreign" had long attached itself to our schools and now it was high time to give evidence to the contrary and relate ourselves to national, social, and civic life. The motivation was admirable, but the implementation absent.

In a major address at the 1943 convention, C. H. Ippel[4] reiterated that "our schools may help our nation by severely maintaining our distinctiveness" and that we "have definite rights of self-determination."[5] In 1952, the Reverend Edward Heerema took issue with James B. Conant's charge that "Christian schools are a divisive force in a democratic society."[6]

In 1962, the theme of Christian Schools and citizenship was back on the agenda. The main speaker at the convention, Frank E. Gaebelein,[7] set forth clearly some fundamental principles and

3. The government withdrew the controversial item, but according to Lyle McBurney, the executive officer of the Ontario Association of Alternative and Independent Schools, the issue has not been laid to rest permanently.

4. Principal of Ebenezer and Kalamazoo Christian High School.

5. *Christian School Annual*, 1943, p. 96.

6. *Christian School Annual*, 1952, pp. 120–130.

7. Headmaster of the Stony Brook School, New York.

methods of teaching citizenship in a Christian school. In addition, he gave timely insight and warned "that we must stop confusing our independence with isolationism, our freedom to teach the faith ... with parochialism and separatism."[8] Gaebelein had wide experience in Christian schools other than those associated with the NUCS. A continuing change toward relating more fully to social and civic life was in the offing. Other speakers — Clarence De Boer, president of the NUCS at that time, and the Reverend William Vander Haak — reflected the same thesis in separate addresses, "No Man Is an Island" and "A Citizen of Two Worlds."

All of the principal speakers at the 1964 convention stressed the need for the Christian school to stick to its authentic biblical foundations while "spilling over to American democracy."[9] Calvin Seerveld observed that "the amicability of Christian schools and the American state is a testimony to the law-abiding respect for government and concern for civic good held by Christian parents. ..." He accented the need of a just state and a free school. De Boer asserted that "our contribution to the American society is preparing our graduates to live the Christian life in this non-Christian society." The Reverend Leonard Verduin made the point that "to educate is to convey the cultural heritage," which could be "culture-creating" or "culture-influencing" — Christianly, of course.

All speakers acknowledged that American democracy is virtually impossible to define to the degree necessary for educational direction and has many faults based on pragmatic ideology, the most obvious being the attempt to omit God. "The Christian school is, as a matter of fact, in contemporary American democracy," said Seerveld, "and we need to be testifying and making a national witness in Washington, D.C. and Ottawa: that all life is religion in operation before God and that only in Jesus Christ is there hope for Anglo American education and democracy."[10]

Financial Aid to Schools in the United States

Pursuant to the legitimate demands for tangible expressions of greater justice, Christian schools and government agencies came

---

8. Christian School *Directory*, 1962, p. 171.
9. All quotations are from the Christian School *Directory*, 1964, pp. 223ff.
10. *Ibid.*, p. 238.

to a near clash in this period over the issue of financial aid for private schools. The complexity of the issue can be sensed when one understands that not only were there strong divergent opinions between advocates of public and private schools, but also there was a heated controversy within private-school groups and to a lesser degree among public-school parties. In this period there was a significant development, namely, a noticeable modification of the traditional position that private schools were not entitled to public support and should militantly oppose any effort to seek it. What follows is a chronological tracing of that modification.

Since the beginning of Christian schools, leaders (with few exceptions) strongly opposed the use of their own money for their schools once these monies became public funds. A. S. De Jong and Mark Fakkema, in their capacities as editor of *Christian Home and School* and general secretary of the NUCS, often voiced their opinions in the 1930s with the familiar strains that the piper calls the tune: government domination would follow and parental interest would erode if public support would be accepted. They offered as evidence the case of Christian education in the Netherlands, which since the 1920s had received financial allotments from the state and was already moving away from the principles it once held and the homes with which it was once closely involved.

There were, however, exceptions to this traditional position. Henry Van Zyl, the first professor in the education department of Calvin College, wrote his doctoral dissertation on public support of British schools, evidencing his conviction on the validity of this idea. In 1933, Ate Dykstra, a representative in the Michigan legislature, introduced a bill authorizing school districts to turn over to parochial (all religious) schools part of the tax money they receive. This bill did not pass, to no one's surprise, but the issue was gaining visibility. Opposing the measure, many Christian-school patrons brought up the argument that there is discipline in sacrifice. Dykstra, like Van Zyl, possibly was ahead of his time by insisting on greater public justice.

The issue then was dormant for several years. In the interim, the question often arose why the Dutch-American Calvinists didn't take a stronger cue from the sagacious theologian-diplomat, Abraham Kuyper, who in the Netherlands had successfully led a movement for a more equitable government financial policy toward Christian schools. Answers suggested that the First Amendment to the United States Constitution places an insurmountable barrier to obtaining a favorable public policy, and that the Christian-school segment of American society was an isolated minority with neither hope nor desire of being heard on this matter. Perhaps another answer is that Kuyper's view on the sovereignty of diverse institutions was not well understood.

Not until 1945 did the issue of governmental policy related to financing significantly surface again. This time the issue was not state aid to private schools, but *federal* aid to private schools. An inherent antifederalism came to blunt expression in the words of a NUCS convention speaker: "Federal subsidy manifests a deplorable lack of faith in our American system."[11] Such remarks had a polarizing affect on the attitudes of Christian-school people. Some, admittedly a minority, applauded what seemed to be a breakthrough in fairer treatment for minorities, educational and religious as well as racial. The reaction of others was to denounce further federal government involvement in elementary and secondary education. Unfortunately, many were confused, assuming that the issues of federal aid and government support or control of private education were synonymous.

The issue of direct financial aid to private schools continued to smolder for several years. It next arose over indirect aid, such as qualifying tuition as a deductible income-tax item. The NUCS, strongly reflecting grass-roots feeling, grew concerned over an obvious inequity: parents who sent their children to parochial schools were receiving deductions on contributions because their contributions were channeled through the church and were not considered tuition. The Internal Revenue Service (IRS) defines tuition as nondeductible. Therefore parents whose children attended NUCS-affiliated schools could not receive deductions, because Christian schools that are governed by parents or associations technically are not parochial schools.

In 1955 the NUCS board of directors set up a committee consisting of Herbert Daverman, Andrew Snoep, and John A. Vander Ark to investigate this matter. The committee had the full cooperation of then-Congressman Gerald R. Ford and met with the deputy director of IRS in Washington, D.C. One fringe benefit grew

---

11. The Reverend Gerrit Hoeksema, 1945 convention address, *Christian School Annual*, p. 65.

out of the meeting. When the committee presented its case of inequity, the deputy director simply said, "The IRS does not *set* tuition." That, the committee felt, was tantamount to saying, "Reduce your tuition and parents will pay fewer tax dollars."

To help his constituents, Ford for several succeeding years sponsored a bill that would make tuition a deductible item. He was also instrumental in having Vander Ark testify to both the Senate finance committee and the House ways and means committee. The outcome was discouraging. NUCS efforts were rigorously opposed by Protestants and Americans United for the Separation of Church and State, a motley assortment of rabid anti-Catholics, humanists, and monastic-minded fellow Christians. Also in opposition, although more quietly, were the National Association of Evangelicals (NAE) and other Christian groups that protested that the Roman Catholic Church would be the greatest beneficiary.

Reflection by NUCS personnel, board members, principals, teachers, and involved parents resulted in a growing consensus concerning a tactic compatible with Christian ethics. Based on the nondirective remark by the deputy director of the IRS, the idea of charging austere tuition was conceived and carried out with qualified success in nearly all IRS districts where Christian schools are located. The concept was that tuition, a bona fide charge, could be set at a low rate, provided school financing was dependent on broadly-based charitable giving.

The NUCS board decided, at its February, 1960, semi-annual meeting, that charging austere tuition was defensible and appointed another committee to draft a policy that could be recommended to schools. Appointed were Louis Van Ess, Walter Hommes, Gordon Kaufman, Gerrit Vander Pol, and Vander Ark. The committee's draft was officially endorsed by the board of directors in August, 1960, as recommended policy for member schools.

Concurrent with this development, the NUCS opened a reconsideration of direct public support in 1958. A study committee from southern California, consisting of Zoetewey, Loren De Wind, and Lawrence Van Noord, was appointed. In a well-reasoned report, the committee recommended taking a firm stand against the use of any funds from government sources for the operation and maintenance of Christian schools, mainly because of the fear of having control shift to government agencies. Recognizing the spiraling cost of education and the burden that it placed on supporters, the committee judged that schools could accept funds to pay for auxiliary services such as transportation, health, and textbooks, and that schools should seek financial relief by means of various tax exemptions, perhaps even on the property of Christian-school patrons. This latter idea reflected a practice current in parts of Canada. The report was referred to member school boards for a one-year study.

By this time (1958) fringe-benefit government aids, as they came to be known, became realities. Among these were payment for experimental programs in science and mathematics, provisions for libraries and laboratories, scholarships, and loans and tuition grants to teachers. This new influx of federal money into education followed quickly the successful Soviet attempt to put its orbiting Sputnik in space. The United States wanted to be second to no one in anything, including education and technology. The benefits of these federal programs (although occasionally difficult to obtain) were available to private schools and their personnel through the National Science Foundation, the National Defense Education Act (NDEA), and the still-operational GI bill, which provided veterans with tuition funds to attend qualified schools of their choice, public or private. The NDEA was definitely discriminatory, since the major benefits were for public schools only.

Meanwhile, the NUCS set up yet another advisory committee on direct government aid. De Boer, the Reverend Adam Persenaire, and Ivan Zylstra recommended in 1960 that no position on direct government aid be taken, since the time was inappropriate. In the committee's opinion there were no scriptural reasons forbidding the use of government funds, but there were practical reasons for being cautious. Furthermore, if public support became available in ways that would not compromise basic teaching, Christian schools should be able to accept that aid as a matter of common justice.

The issue fortunately did not rest. At this juncture another in a long series of committees was mandated specifically to answer the question: Is it right or wrong *in principle* for the Christian-school constituency to accept government aid? This question assumed, of course, was that there would be a clear, workable definition of government aid, which in a sense was a misnomer. The real issue was to what degree Christian-school supporters (and other nonpublic school patrons) would be allowed the use of money that they paid in taxes to educate their own children in keeping with their convictions of what education should be. J. Herman Fles, Cornelius Jaarsma, William Van Rees, Cornelius Van Valkenburg, and Nicholas Yff constituted the new committee. They made three recommendations: that government aid is sound historically and in principle, that our Christian school system has a right to government aid, and that Christian-school constituents should actively defend and exercise that right.[12]

Five grounds were given for these conclusions, the main one embracing parental responsibility and rights in education. Others were the equal protection by law and courts to uphold their rights, the recognition that the exercise of religious rights cannot be realized in a secular school, that the Christian school is an integral part of the democratic community, and that the freedom of choice is contingent on a rightful proportionate share of taxes levied on all citizens.

The NUCS House of Delegates, at the annual meeting at Purdue University in 1962, adopted the first two recommendations, but declined to adopt the third, which presumably would have made it necessary to set up stratagems to acquire government aid. Donald Oppewal evaluated the situation in an article with a striking metaphor from football: "Off the Bleachers and Onto the Field."[13] Although disappointed that the delegates did not adopt all of the recommendations, he detected two significant trends that emerged: "The NUCS is taking a more aggressive leadership role within the system (more like a captain of the team than a waterboy), and notice is being served on the American public that Christian school supporters want to be responsible members of American society, making their contribution and getting their rights."

Oppewal rightly observed further that the logic of the stand forced the NUCS into action. "A principle not acted upon, or fought for, is a dead principle, and will be relegated to the wastebasket of history."[14]

Other individuals and organizations were beginning to make

12. Christian School *Directory*, 1962, p. 159.
13. *The Reformed Journal*, September, 1962, p. 3.
14. *Ibid.*, p. 4.

their contributions known on this issue. Notable among individuals was Edwin H. Palmer, who strongly presented the case for support in a mimeographed paper, "Freedom and Equity in Dutch Education." One of the influential organizations that emerged was Citizens for Educational Freedom (CEF), a national organization with chapters in the states as well. John Vanden Berg of Calvin College was the board chairman. CEF did much to form coalitions of all religious schools to secure parents' rights in education.

In 1963 the NUCS officially continued to take a "no-action" stand on federal aid on the grounds that Christian schools had not demonstrated a convincing need for such aid. "Nevertheless, should legislation be enacted, the NUCS strongly advises that the granting of it solely to public schools would constitute discrimination and an infringement on the liberty protected by the Fourteenth Amendment."[15]

Clarence J. De Boer, M.D.

Not all Christian-school leaders were persuaded that government aid was good and defensible. Articulate among these was De Boer, a prominent surgeon and a gentle Christian with deep convictions, who also, incidentally, was an anti-smoking and anti-football campaigner. Moreover, he was a member of the NUCS board of directors from 1959 to 1965, serving as president from 1960 to 1965. In formal addresses as well as in discussion forums, he spelled out well the arguments against seeking funds. His conviction is summarized in his own words, "It [aid to private schools] is unworkable in terms of American political experience and would have a corrosive effect on our spiritual foundations and commitments." Although the mild-mannered De Boer presided with emi-

15. Christian School *Directory*, 1963, p. 150.

nent fairness, his leadership explains in part the deliberate progress in getting "off the bleachers and onto the field" in this crucial area.

In 1963 the NUCS, for the first time, endorsed the issuance of certificates (vouchers) to parents.[16] Then, stating unequivocally "that we cannot surrender our right to education in harmony with religious principle," the NUCS urged its districts to become more active in supporting or opposing legislation that affected Christian schools.[17] In keeping with this stance the NUCS set up a new position, secretary of school relations, and appointed to that post Philip Elve, recognized as an extremely competent administrator in Christian-school affairs.

Although at this time there was no separate Government Relations Department (it was set up in 1966 and Zylstra was appointed administrator), Elve became deeply involved in government-related matters. A ground swell of interest arose in austere tuition. The NUCS gave counsel to inquiring schools as well as parents and became a clearing-house for problem cases. The concept seemed for a while to be the most practical scheme to give tuition-paying parents relief, albeit in the form of indirect government aid. The practice, unfortunately, was not consistently administered in all IRS districts. Moreover, local IRS offices began to feel the loss of revenue and, lacking a directive or a precedent-setting court decision to honor the concept, local auditors in many instances disallowed deductions as filed. A 1959 court case in California, *De Jong v. Commissioner of Internal Revenue Service*, dealt the severest blow to the concept. The ruling not only disallowed taxpayer De Jong a deduction on tuition payments, but also declared that the full cost of education (De Jongs' contribution exceeded that) was the criterion determining nondeductibility of parental payment. Based on these experiences, the practice of charging austere tuition steadily faded out of existence.

This period of history, 1943 – 1965, evidenced a major shift from strong opposition to state involvement in Christian-school financ-

16. The central idea, as it pertains to elementary and secondary schools, was first proposed by Milton Friedman in 1955; it embodies the same principle as that of the GI bill, which permits the purchase of educational service at a qualified school of one's choice. The majority of beneficiaries of the GI bill used their opportunities on the postsecondary level.

17. Christian School *Directory*, 1963, p. 150.

ing to a position of qualified support. The citizen and Christian educational institutions, it was generally well agreed by 1965, must not abandon political responsibilities in the pursuit of justice and righteousness. The struggle for justice continued.

Tax credit, officially approved as a desirable tax-incentive plan, was overshadowed by the Elementary and Secondary Education Act of 1965, which promised peripheral but significant financial help to Christian schools and personnel.

Informed readers may wonder why no account is given of the struggle for state aid in states where Christian schools are concentrated. The author simply advances the caveat that the early sixties were a tooling-up period and that a more meaningful account should appear in a subsequent book. The situation in Canada is different.

The Canadian Scenario

The seedbed for developing vital relationships between Christian schools and governmental units and obtaining funding in Canada had been prepared long before this period. Actually, the story begins with the British North America (BNA) act (1867), which created a dual school system — Protestant and Catholic (separate) — and assigned the responsibility for education to the provinces. It is significant to remember that the BNA act provided rights and privileges only for denominational schools if they were in existence by law before confederation. Steadily, as secularism made inroads into Canadian society, the Protestant system became designated public. Protestants who for reasons of principle wanted to operate schools of their choice were saddled with a twofold handicap: their schools were not recognized as schools and they were not supported with government funds, part of which had been extracted from them through taxation.

Naturally Christian-school supporters were highly displeased that monies collected from all taxpayers for the support of education should be directed only to public schools and through grade ten to separate schools. They felt the burden of unequal educational opportunities. Fortunately, the BNA act, while safeguarding the dual school system, did not forbid provinces to tolerate another system, for example, an independent system. Those interested in independent, including Christian, schools thoughtfully began first to seek legal recognition of their schools and then press for educational grants.

Christian and all independent school leaders set up a sort of pattern to gain these ends. They curried the respect of political and educational officials in the provinces. They formed coalitions of independent schools and prepared briefs, largely to promote awareness and understanding of their schools. Since education is a provincial responsibility and each province has a peculiar history of the development of governmental relations to independent schools, it is necessary to treat provinces separately. Also, to get a proper perspective on such development, one really needs to go beyond 1965. Thus, we stretch the end parameter of this period.

Ontario

In Ontario, change in provincial policy with respect to government support is amazingly slow. Although Ontario Christian schools comply with provincial regulations, they receive no financial aid. That does not mean that patrons were idle. Some Christian schools exerted individual efforts. Hamilton Christian School Society, for example, tried in 1962 to form a separate (non-Catholic) school board with the hope of receiving tax money for school support. The government flatly denied the request on the grounds that the effort did not comport with the interest of the BNA act.

The Ontario Alliance of Christian Schools (NUCS District 10) was also active. It set up an arm, the Committee on Justice and Liberty, and engaged counselor John Olthuis to prepare briefs and other literature. Henry Nieman, sometime local (London) school-board president and officer of the alliance, in a May 25, 1982, letter to the author, wrote:

> Our time was spent contacting [Christian] school boards to make local presentations to their politicians by inviting them to our schools and making them aware of our existence and the contributions [our schools make] to the respective communities they serve. As a committee we made a presentation to the governing party as well as to the opposition parties. The Prime Minister and other influential people in government were contacted and kept informed. During that time we made a lot of headway as to awareness and determination of our existence, but we never did get the grant.

Two government reports on education followed in quick succession, the Hall-Dennis Report in 1968 and the Mackay Report in 1969. The first gave a ray of hope when it called for equal opportunity for all Ontario youth and cited the United Nations Declaration of Human Rights (p. 11), which affirms the prior right of parents to choose the kind of education their children shall receive. The final position of the commission, however, snuffed out the ray of hope when it asserted that commitment to the public and separate school systems satisfied the requirements of the constitution.

The Mackay Report, issued by the Committee on Religious Education in the Public School, provided the potential for intensifying the conflict between public and independent schools while finding the program of religious education to be "unsatisfactory and inefficient for the purpose of developing a truly educated and cultivated person" (p. 71). The committee, according to the Ontario Alliance, showed a "total lack of respect for other than public schools." Olthuis criticized the report sharply in a brief to the Ontario government in 1969. He noted particularly that the committee, in the Mackay Report, "rejected as destructive of our great democracy" (p. 26) government support of parochial and private schools. Olthuis assailed the committee for violating its own "don't-indoctrinate" rule by making inevitable "indoctrination of humanism."

Although no progress on equal educational opportunity can be claimed, the efforts of the alliance will not likely go down as unrewarding. One notable benefit that came out of this confrontation was that the alliance gave leadership in rethinking and reformulating statements on the purpose of education. A key statement from that literature is that "all education is religious in character."

The torch for seeking freedom of choice in education is now being carried by a new coalition called the Ontario Association of Alternative and Independent Schools. Lyle McBurney is its executive secretary.

Alberta

"When Alberta became a province in 1905, the dual system of public and separate schools was supported by the government in

Ottawa."[18] In 1943 the independent schools in Alberta were already under the School Act, which imposed regulations on teacher certification, building requirements (square footage), and teacher-pupil ratio.

As the number of independent schools increased, regulations became more sweeping. By 1946, provincial regulations more explicitly governed the permission to establish private schools, the program of studies, and inspection by the minister of education. Prior to 1961, attendance at a private school was recognized in the School Act as an excuse for not attending a public school. Then came a period of changes.

J. B. Ludwig cites four developments that account for changes. (The following data are extracted from his study.) First was the formation of the Association of Private Schools in 1958. It was instrumental in presenting the views of its member schools to the provincial government, asserted the rights of parents in education, and submitted a brief to the cabinet, asking for equal treatment of public schools in a number of areas.

Second, in 1959 the Royal Commission on Education (Cameron) presented a report that devoted about one page to private schools. It voiced no objection to them if they provide a service at the expense of their supporters and maintain provincial standards of education. Unintentionally the majority report, while defending the rights of taxpayers whose taxes are assigned to separate schools against their will, gave comfort to any taxpayer whose taxes are assigned without his determination.

Significantly, too, a member of the commission, George Cormack of Edmonton, submitted a minority report forcefully supporting "parental rights to control not only the financing but also the philosophy of education to which the child will be subjected." He criticized Alberta education as being "the only democratic institution in the province where pluralism is not recognized or espoused."[19]

Third, the Christian-school movement *came into the kingdom for such a time as this.* Supporters of Christian schools became

18. J. B. Ludwig, "Control and Financing of Private Education in Alberta: The Role of Parents, Church, and State." Unpublished thesis, submitted in partial fulfillment of requirements for the master of arts degree at the University of Alberta, Edmonton, 1970.

19. *Ibid.*, p. 37.

very "active in a number of organizations in an effort to obtain recognition and support from the provincial treasury."[20] They were active in the Association of Private Schools, the Social Credit Party, and the Christian Action Foundation. The list of participants is too long to mention here but one ought at least to be acknowledged: F. H. Verhoef, valiant defender of Christian education in Calgary and secretary of NUCS District 11.

In 1968 the NUCS District 11 engaged the Gunderson Public Relations firm of Calgary to evaluate its public image and to make recommendations for a more effective organizational structure. Harald Gunderson highly commended the district and its schools for their philosophy, sacrifice, and determination. "The time has come to tell your story,"[21] he reported, and laid out a plan of action for them.

The NUCS district prepared a brief in connection with the proposed new School Act in which it recommended that independent (the new name for private) schools be recognized through legislation and that grants to such schools be equal to 75 percent of capital and operational grants to public schools.

The fourth development leading to better recognition and status of independent schools, according to Ludwig, was well-timed political action. The activity of supporters of Christian education in community and party politics brought results. L. A. Fleming, a member of the Social Credit Party who represented Calgary West, presented a motion to the 1966 Alberta legislature that called for equality based on parental rights and financial assistance to private schools teaching the Alberta curriculum. The motion carried and government action implemented it in 1967 when a one-hundred-dollar grant per pupil for approved private schools was introduced. By adopting this measure, Alberta established a precedent in government support of independent schools.

Subsequently the government increased the grant until it escalated to 70 percent of the cost of public education.

Manitoba

When Manitoba became a province it precipitated a crisis in educational matters. The new legislature refused to recognize the

20. *Ibid.*, p. 40.
21. *Ibid.*, p. 41.

provision in the BNA act with respect to separate schools and made public schools the only legal educational entity. Public schools alone received funding.

After a long and complex struggle, involving debates on federal versus provincial control of education and the relative importance of state, church, and parental voice in establishing educational policy, there was a breakthrough in 1966. The provincial legislature instituted a shared service program then, which, according to John Doornbos, principal of Calvin Christian School in Winnipeg, gradually increased to include not only bus transportation but also public-school instruction in home economics and industrial arts for private-school children.

The Manitoba Federation of Independent Schools made a broad-based approach to public-school boards, members of the legislative assemblies, and cabinet ministers, and in 1977 obtained a per-pupil grant of $350 per year. This has since increased.

British Columbia

The history of independent education in British Columbia is a fascinating story of a struggle for identity. The first issue, according to Beatrice Vander Heiden, a teacher at Pacific Christian who researched the subject and wrote a paper on it for a class at the University of Victoria, focuses on the *legal* recognition of private schools. Back in 1894, writing on the history of the province, Alexander Begg claimed "there are no 'separate schools' in British Columbia."

Vander Heiden points out that in Begg's time separate schools were indeed operating. "In the earliest days of colonization all education was denominational and sporadic. [Missionaries established schools in western Canada during the rule of the Hudson Bay Company.] Obviously he [Begg] was referring to the fact that no legally recognized separate school system was in existence."[22]

In British Columbia, as in all of Canada, the debate started with the Act of Union of 1841, which provided for a separate school system in Upper and Lower Canada. It found further expression in the BNA act in 1867, which gave the provinces the exclusive

22. "History of Private Education in British Columbia." Unpublished paper, 1976.

right to make laws in relation to education and gave to denominational schools whatever rights and privileges they had by law in the province at the union (see section 93).

When British Columbia joined the Confederation in 1871, the new provincial legislature hastened to adopt a Public School Act (1872) that would establish a strictly nonsectarian school system. This made British Columbia the first province (Manitoba was second) to have a single system. "To allay the fears of many that the schools would be 'Godless' schools," writes Vander Heiden, "the recommendation was made that the school day be opened and closed with a prescribed prayer and that the Ten Commandments be taught."[23]

The controversy brought on by the Public School Act of 1872 raged for many years. It did not deter citizens, however, from seeking alternatives to public education. The struggle to gain recognition assumed a new approach following World War II, when the number of independent schools increased. The approach was called "the thin edge of the wedge." During the forties and fifties, in response to pressure from taxpayers, the government granted to independent schools free textbooks, health service, and pupil transportation. Such action was based on the idea that the state should protect the child. Soon thereafter, in 1957, municipalities exempted private-school properties from taxation. Then a new argument surfaced, namely, that independent schools performed a service for the benefit of society. In addition to the foregoing benefits, private schools received one other recognition — the permissive assurance that attendance at a private school was a safeguard against truancy.

Meanwhile independent schools multiplied and costs of education spiraled. The time was ripe for a new approach, that of coalition and confrontation. Divergent groups interested in religious education — Roman Catholics, Anglicans, NUCS schools, Jews, Mennonites, and Lutherans — met in 1964 to discuss common problems and ambitions. As a result of this meeting the Federation of Independent School Associations (FISA) was founded in 1966. "The aim of FISA was to create a political climate hos-

23. *Ibid.*, p. 11.

pitable to the existence of independent schools and supportive of their public funding."[24]

This called for coordination of many efforts of disseminating information and political activism. The new organization appointed Gerard Ensing, then principal of Vancouver Christian School, as fulltime executive director to coordinate the efforts of the federation and to serve as its official spokesman.

The federation prepared a brief in 1967, a historic first, to the Honorable L. R. Petersen, minister of education at the time. NUCS District 12 also prepared a brief to try to get a cabinet hearing. The road was not easy. "The climate was in fact hostile," Ensing averred. The federation, however, brought about a radical change through writing campaigns, radio phone-in programs, and numerous speaking engagements.

The time ripened for political action. "The climate had changed from being completely hostile to independent schools in the mid-sixties, to the point where even the New Democratic Party (NDA) [traditionally opposed to recognizing independent schools] in 1975 was willing to provide services to independent schools short of paying direct grants for actual academic services."[25] The Social Credit Party, having made an about-face by accepting a policy favoring the recognition and funding of independent schools, came to power that year and confirmed its campaign promise in speeches from the throne in 1976 and 1977.

That latter year the legislature passed Bill 33, which became a landmark in the history of education in British Columbia. This bill authorized funding for institutions in terms of the number of pupils they serve. Among those who should receive acknowledgment for championing the ideology of multiple alternatives in education is Patrick McGeer, who became minister of education.

The history of developments in recognition and public support of independent education in Canada and the United States is not identical. However, in reviewing the literature on the subject, one

---

24. L. W. Downey, "The Anatomy of a Policy Decision, B. C.'s Bill 33 — The Independent School Support Act." Unpublished paper, University of British Columbia, Vancouver, 1979.

25. Gerard Ensing, "History of the Federation of Independent Schools." A report to constituent schools and the public.

is deeply impressed with the great common bond that exists, especially considering arguments in favor of recognition and support.[26]

High on the list are the concepts embraced by the terms *equality* and *justice*. The outstanding feature of our North American nations is their pluralistic character. People differ vastly in principles they hold dear. Public recognition and support of private schools would resolve a multitude of persistent problems that stem from that fact: the separation of family and state, the relation of religion to education, and freedom of choice in education. Moreover, compulsory attendance, without enabling support, is an injustice.

A second category of arguments in favor of recognition and support deals with the contributions that private — in this instance Christian — schools make. They contribute significantly to society as a whole, to inculcations of moral and spiritual values (an insurmountable problem in neutral schools), and to freedom. A pluralistic system allows parents, teachers, and pupils ways to exercise their personal and academic freedoms.

A third category of arguments in favor of recognition and support may be classified as practical. Christian schools save taxpayers much money. Partial payments to private schools or to families would induce more people to use such schools. They would bear part of the cost of education and thus reduce the taxpayers' obligation.

Finally, a common mind exists generally among Christian-school patrons of both nations with respect to state control of education. They believe that some control is inevitable, with or without public support, and acceptable if administered without bias. The areas of control are determining standards of achievement, minimum qualifications for teachers, and building standards.

26. Ludwig devotes fourteen pages (52–65) to a summary of arguments in favor and in opposition.

7

Curriculum: Input and Output

The preparation of Christian instructional materials has always had high priority among Christian-school advocates. It was one of the main objectives in founding the National Union of Christian Schools (NUCS) in 1920 and has appeared on its agenda ever since. Consistency requires that to teach and learn Christianly there must be harmony between materials and teacher. The difference between secular and Christian schools, Christian-school advocates believe, is brought out explicitly in the curriculum and the textbooks.

Writing and publishing such different materials, which for many years were called Christian-school textbooks, were pursued with varying speed and approaches. In the early history there were expectant glances toward the Netherlands, in the hope that some materials could be translated and with minor adaptations made suitable for American schools. Cooperation with other Protestant groups such as the Lutherans was also investigated. The possibility of making an arrangement with secular textbook publishers (especially of reader series, by substituting suitable Christian materials for some of the blatantly humanistic pieces) was another hope of many Christian educators.

On the premise that fellow saints need one another, the NUCS explored once again in 1946 and 1948 the feasibility of working with other Protestant schools on curriculum materials. Conferences were held with representatives of the Lutheran Church-Missouri Synod, namely, A. C. Stellhorn and William Kramer. Christian textbooks in science were a particular concern. A report on this matter disappointingly ends with the familiar cliche: Nothing came of it. The NUCS conferees did, however, receive a manuscript for an eighth-grade reader, which, to the surprise of no one, was weighted with accounts of Martin Luther. No joint effort came of that. It did, however, provide a stronger rationale for preparing the Pilot Series.

The NUCS made further contacts with Mennonites and Seventh-Day Adventists. Both practical and ideological reasons prevented further pursuit of joint ventures. The upshot of such conferences was that the Protestant groups decided to go their separate ways. As the NUCS educational program developed, other groups made considerable use of its publications, as evidenced in the sale of materials to a wide range of Protestant schools.

In the late 1940s John A. Van Bruggen also investigated the possibility of making arrangements with a few major publishers to modify secular texts for use in Christian schools. He proposed to the Macmillan Company an adaptation of the Gates Readers, comparable to the Cathedral (Catholic) Series published by Scott, Foresman Company, and also a special edition of Ginn and Company's science series. A negative shock came when the latter company stated its condition for publishing an adaptation of its series, namely, a guarantee to purchase fifty thousand to seventy-five thousand books. Further, a proposal to Singer Publishing Corporation for an adapted language textbook in cooperation with Lutherans fizzled out.

These pursuits having failed, Christian-school leaders plodded along with dedication and hope for better days. They managed, however, to pioneer a few "distinctively different" books. Among those published before 1943 were B. J. Bennink's *Sketches from Church History* (1926); Richard Postma's *Sacred History Outlines of O.T.* (c. 1935); Catherine Vos's *Child's Story Bible* (1935); *Christian Interpretation of American History* (1928) by Garrett Heyns and Garrit Roelofs; *Excelsior Readers* (1919 and 1920) by Gerhardus Bos; *God's Great Out of Doors* series (1938 and 1939) by Marian Schoolland; and the *Pupil Bible Study* series (1935–1940) by Andrew Blystra, Mark Fakkema, and Nicholas Yff.

Three seemingly insurmountable difficulties were frequently pinpointed: first, the persistent question, What counts as "Christian"?; second, a limited reservoir of competent writers; third, pro-

J.C. Lobbes

duction costs beyond the ability of schools of the NUCS to pay.

The year 1943 will go down in Christian-school history as a strategic one in this concern. It marks a beginning of a renewal and a redirection of the Christian-textbook or curriculum-development program, as it came to be known. The NUCS board of directors posed an important question to its member schools that year: What services to member schools should the NUCS accentuate? Already sensitive to the need for more and better instructional aids and wanting an authentic answer from the field, from the whole spectrum of Christian-school educators, the NUCS board set up a new body and mandated it to make an assessment.[1]

The committee commendably examined the background of this concern and found it had a long history. It assumed that the NUCS board had been stimulated over the years by papers such as the one presented by Principal J. C. Lobbes, then from Edgerton, Minnesota, at the 1942 annual convention.[2] Lobbes explicated the relation between general and special revelation and pointed out that,

considering God's general revelation as revealing God Himself, this required an acknowledgment of Him
1. as the Creator of the material universe (the cosmological aspect);
2. through the intelligence, order, design, and purpose in His creation (the teleological aspect);
3. in the course of human events (history);

1. Previously, the NUCS had a textbook committee. This body made preliminary decisions on critical areas for special Christian textbooks and, with the board's approval, commissioned individuals to write materials with a relatively free hand. The reason for creating another committee is not clear from the minutes and other official sources. It appears that teachers were clamoring the loudest for more textbooks and the board decided to give "professionals" a chance to contribute some guidance in working out a fuller service program to schools in educational matters.

2. The title is "School Branches Viewed as Branches on the Tree of God's Self-Revelation." *Christian School Annual*, 1942, pp. 82ff.

4. in the moral consciousness of man; and last but not least,
5. in man's aesthetic nature, reflecting Him who is the source of all things beautiful.

All of these aspects cried out for further application in the Christian-school classroom. The paper pointed out specific ways to teach these concepts, and by extension, emphasized the importance of materials to embody these perspectives.

The education committee was appointed in 1943. It consisted of the Reverend Herman Bel, Walter De Jong, John De Vries, Cornelius Zylstra, and Henry Kuiper, a group that had ideas of its own and also was open to better ideas as it faithfully surveyed the field. The answer it gave to the board was well-documented: get on with a more refined instructional aid program. "Give us Christian textbooks," was the message the committee heard clearly from member schools.

The implementation of the study was not rushed; the usual alibis about shortages of money and writers were given. In fact, three years passed from the time the study was begun until the board crystallized plans to prepare for an accelerated program of publishing educational materials. The board could scarcely be accused of rashness in such matters. At the 1946 annual meeting in Pella, Iowa, the board tested the waters among constituents. Almost unanimously the delegates affirmed the board's earlier position, giving evidence of supporting a stepped-up program. Curriculum development became a high priority.

The issue regarding who should handle the editing and publishing of Christian-school textbooks naturally surfaced. Fakkema's competence and achievement in promotional work stood out in sharp relief, but his qualifications in producing educational materials were less evident. The board favored the creation of a new position and proceeded with the appointment of an educational secretary while retaining Fakkema as promotional secretary. There should be no doubt about Fakkema's undaunted commitment to the preparation of Christian textbooks. Representative of his convictions on this matter is a comment that appears in the 1943 *Christian School Annual:*

Each school has two teachers—the teacher behind the teacher's desk and the teacher on the pupil's desk ... $500,000 is spent annually for teachers, so that our covenant youth may receive something different from the public schools. This difference falls short if our basic texts are identical.[3]

After bandying about the selection of an educational secretary for some time, the board decided to appoint Zylstra, member of the strategic education committee, editor of *Christian Home and School*, and principal of Baxter Christian School in Grand Rapids. He declined the appointment but agreed later to serve as educational editor. He served well in this position for one year and accomplished much, including the editing of the *Course of Study for Christian Schools*, 1947.[4]

John A. Van Bruggen.

Van Bruggen, principal of Oakdale Christian School in Grand Rapids, Michigan, was the board's choice that year to be educational secretary. He too was an ardent proponent of Christian-school textbooks. A synopsis of his views appears in an article he wrote for *Christian Home and School:*

> The textbook of the present day is a tremendous force in the education of youth ... [modern educational authorities and writers] regard the evolutionary hypothesis as truth and assume that every pupil does or should learn to accept it as such. ... Our Christian

3. P. 51.
4. The following contributed to this benchmark publication: Henry Schultze, "A Philosophy of Christian Education"; Postma, "Bible Study"; Barney Peterson, "Arithmetic"; Leonard R. Haan, "Language and Spelling"; Zylstra, "History"; Richard Tolsma, "Citizenship and Government"; Schoolland, "Elementary Science"; Henry Bengelink, "Health and Safety and Service"; Grace Brink, "Music"; and Fakkema, "History of Our Christian Schools."

schools are using these textbooks in spite of the fact that their
approach very subtly undermines the precious truths our conse-
crated teachers attempt to convey to our children. . . . Today, when
the textbook is regarded as a very important and effective educational instrument, this practice may no longer be tolerated.[5]

By the time Van Bruggen was appointed in 1947, the board had
not fully articulated the relationships of the promotional and educational secretaryships. Should they be coordinate with equal
and direct responsibilities to the board or should one person have
responsibility for coordinating tasks? Considering the independent personalities of the two principals, and believing that having
one person in charge is a good principle of administration, the
board redefined the jobs and gave Van Bruggen the title of educational director with a broad mandate, including coordination of
staff activities.

Having more than one cook in the kitchen appeared to be a
severe problem, but a resolution was near. The stage was set, as
already indicated, for Fakkema to accept the challenge of undertaking a new function with the National Association of Christian
Schools (NACS). Through strong and stable leadership, such as
that given by Postma, president of the NUCS board at this time,
the administrative structure was refined, and for the first time in
its history the NUCS became known as more than a promotional
organization.

Two other staff appointments at this time ought to be acknowledged in view of the strategic services each rendered and the long
tenure of the appointees. They were Beth Merizon, who succeeded
Zylstra as education editor and became associate editor of *Christian Home and School,* and Betty De Vries, secretary to the director. Among the accomplishments of Merizon in her twenty-six-
year tenure are the editing of *Story of the Old World* by John
De Bie and prime responsibility in preparing the three-volume
Pilot Series in Literature. Besides doing sundry functions of an
executive secretary for twenty-two years, De Vries was the coordinator of *The Children's Hymnbook* and *Hymns for Youth.*

Van Bruggen worked tirelessly for six intense years to give
educational matters greater prominence. Besides favoring a more

5. September, 1948, p. 9.

Betty De Vries.

Beth Merizon.

aggressive textbook program, he brought to his new position a good rationale for a comprehensive service program. It was encompassed in six points: promotion, study, research, publication, conference, and service. These were not unfamiliar facets of the NUCS, but Van Bruggen brought new emphases to these NUCS activities by classifying the services and pressing for their development.

Philosophy of Christian Education

At this time in Christian-school history the subject of an educational philosophy was of increasing importance. An accelerated program of educational publications was in the offing, and naturally, a written statement of the philosophical basis of Christian education was utterly essential. In the previous decade the issue was debated with vigor by thinkers such as Cornelius Van Til, William H. Jellema, John De Boer, and A. S. De Jong. Opinions were by no means unanimous. Van Til, for example, placed a strong antithesis between the Christian faith and non-Christian learning. Jellema revealed his point of view in the language of *civitas dei* (city of God) and *civitas mundi* (city of the world or city of man). He stressed that Christians rightly have access to universal knowledge. The core of agreement among philosophers was that Christian schools are a natural outgrowth of the Calvinistic view of life; all participants in the discussion objected to a dualistic division of life into the "secular" and the "spiritual," to use the familiar language of the time.

The NUCS education committees in operation from 1943 to 1965 worked steadily on the writing of a generally acceptable philosophy of Christian education. The first product was the statement written by Henry Schultze and contained in the 1947 *Course of Study*. While appreciative of its originating qualities, many teachers felt that it was neither sufficiently complete nor final, as well as too theoretical and theological a basis for curriculum development.

To placate many educators Cornelius Jaarsma was enlisted to write a more complete paper discussing the philosophy of Christian education. The education committee found Jaarsma's "statement in its present form not simple enough for the average teacher to comprehend."[6] The NUCS enlisted the help of Calvin College to prepare a basic philosophical statement through the committee on cooperation between Calvin College and the NUCS. This committee was composed of Bert P. Bos, Lambert Flokstra, Henry Stob, Jaarsma, Jellema, and Van Bruggen. Jaarsma was prolific in writing and speaking on this subject, accenting particularly personality development through schooling. He stressed maturation, the growth of the child (educand), as the highest objective of Christian education. Some others were more inclined to emphasize subject matter, arguing that it reveals God. After a few years of critiquing and other efforts, and unable to reach consensus, the committee advised the NUCS to abandon the effort to have one official statement and to have several, each writer assuming personal responsibility for his own statement.

Despite the difficulties and the disappointments of attempting to produce a statement that was agreeable to all, hard decisions had to be made on what is different, or rather distinctive, about Christian education. At the pioneering stage two questions pressed for an answer: What is Christian and what is education?

No group has a monopoly on that noble word *Christian*, and Christians do not all agree on what is Christian in or about education. Moreover, education has been going on since mankind was created and received the cultural mandate, but how differently Christians apply that truth! Specific questions had to be raised:

6. NUCS education committee minutes, April 8, 1950, article 25.

What must a school do? What subjects taught in which ways are most conducive to preparing children for life? For what life? What are the basic needs of young people created in the image of God? What methodologies are most effective and in harmony with answers to these questions?

Behind such questions and the persons by whom a statement on Christian philosophy was requested, was the all-embracing one: What is the purpose of life? It can surely be said that all who approached the problem agreed that the answer is found in the way God reveals Himself, particularly in His inscripturated Word. It is the proper norm for man's life and sets the goals for living and, by extension, for education that is awkwardly referred to as preparation for life. All agreed that since there are God-given absolutes, it is axiomatic that an educational system must give pupils the potential for living a life in fellowship with Him. Henry Zylstra phrased it succinctly: "... give pupils more to be Christian with." Within the Reformed community, educational philosophers have not always fully agreed on what to accentuate in a statement on the philosophy of Christian education. Disagreements among the pioneers are better understood now with the insights provided by later writers on Christian philosophy or theology of education, such as N. Henry Beversluis,[7] Nicholas Wolterstorff, and Donald Oppewal.

The pooled effort was not completely dissipated, however. By 1953 the NUCS was pleased to publish a booklet by Jaarsma and J. L. De Beer, *Toward a Philosophy of Christian Education.* It was given official endorsement but, as the title indicates, was not considered a final statement. It had, however, immediate and long-range influence on the work of the curriculum writers. Other interested parties, one of whom was the Reverend Arthur De Kruyter, were stimulated to write on the subject. His doctoral thesis, "A Christian Philosophy of Education of the Christian Day Schools in America," was mimeographed and used for some time in college classes for teacher education.

Van Bruggen indicated in 1948 that the preparation of a fully satisfying statement may require "several years." It definitely has.

7. *Christian Philosophy of Education* (Grand Rapids: CSI, 1971) and *Toward a Theology of Education* (occasional papers from Calvin College), vol. 1, no. 1, February, 1981.

The lack of a single clear, concise, comprehensive statement of the philosophy did not, however, preclude the publication of curriculum guides and Christian textbooks. Authors and editors provided brief statements in various fields of subject matter, all of which were within the parameters of a general philosophical statement.

To pursue further developments in the preparation and application of Christian education would take us well beyond 1965. An anticipatory reference, however, can be made to a few writers whose major contributions grew out of these early efforts. Bersluis received a grant from the Christian School Educational Foundation (CSEF) in 1964 to assist him in graduate work with the view to writing a published statement on the philosophy of Christian education. Oppewal and Wolterstorff of Calvin College also continued to write about this basic concern.[8]

Publications in Van Bruggen's Tenure

Several educational publications were on the drawing boards and some were completed during Van Bruggen's tenure. A songbook for young children was on the anticipatory list for several years. The publication of *Let Youth Praise Him*[9] was brought to completion with a one-thousand-dollar gift from the central council of parent-teacher associations of Grand Rapids. *What Shall We Play?* by Kay Hager Tiemersma and *The Church in History* by B. K. Kuiper were completed. The Pilot Series in Literature, edited by Merizon, Gertrude Haan, and Alice Fenenga, was in the conceptual stage. *Story of the Old World* by De Bie was all but ready for printing at the next changing of the guard, when Van Bruggen and the Reverend Edward Heerema were succeeded by John A. Vander Ark and Sidney Dykstra. But before pursuing that development, a new factor must be understood.

There was evidence that one major difficulty with respect to publishing textbooks was diminishing, namely, the doubt that the system could find authors with ability to write quality material. For the moment there was no apparent solution to the third prob-

8. See the Bibliography.

9. The compiling committee consisted of the Reverend H. J. Kuiper, Tena Bajema, Trena Haan, Nella Mierop, and Henrietta Van Laar.

lem, the lack of a stable source of income to finance a continuing program.

The Trials of Publication

The preparation of materials for use in Christian schools had its trials, frustrations, and sometimes inexcusable austerity. When B. K. Kuiper was requested in 1945 to write the book on church history he contracted for the meager remuneration of five hundred dollars, to be paid when the manuscript was completed. At one stage he asked for a fifty-dollar advance, which the board rather tersely denied, offering as defense the contracted agreement. Out of harmony with that judgment, a member of the staff personally advanced him the money, which Kuiper repaid when he received his remuneration. A few years after the book was published, friends of Kuiper prodded him to ask for a more gratuitous payment. The board relented on its erstwhile legalistic stand and gave him an additional fifteen hundred dollars.

The arrangement with De Bie was more liberal. The West Side Christian School of Grand Rapids granted him a year's leave of absence, thus keeping his contract intact. The NUCS, from the CSEF, reimbursed the school for De Bie's service as author.

A Foundation Is Created

The NUCS board, reflecting upon a few years' experience in the preparation of Christian textbooks, soon became aware that sponsoring such educational projects would require an extensive and dependable source of income. There was not enough money in the union's funds, and there was no arrangement for the maintenance of a separate fund for carrying out the job. Consequently, the board of the NUCS recommended to the convention of 1948 that it create an educational foundation. The concept was the brainchild of Jacob Van't Hof, president of the union board at this time, who had previous involvement with a prototype, a trust-type foundation of the National Funeral Directors' Association. Of the latter he had been a member and president. The recommendation was overwhelmingly approved at the 1948 convention in Muskegon, Michigan, over the vocal objections of a few delegates who thought the emphasis should be on teacher preparation rather than on curriculum materials.

As a foundation was being established, a voluntary committee under the leadership of James La Grand conducted a nationwide campaign to raise $100,000. The response was gratifying. Gifts and pledges amounted to $124,000. Of this amount, $50,000 was set aside for an administration and service building for the NUCS at 865 Twenty-eighth Street, S.E., in Grand Rapids, and the balance was placed in a reserve fund. The actual cost of the building was only $60,000, in reality a gift of the foundation.

A foundation needs a founder. For an initial gift of five hundred dollars George Broodman, an ardent and faithful supporter of Christian education, became the founder of the CSEF and a charter trustee. In consultation with the NUCS board and in harmony with state and federal laws pertaining to foundations, he selected other trustees of the foundation. Nearly all were current or past members of the NUCS board of directors. The charter trustees were Herman Baker, Aldrich Evenhouse, Henry Hoving, La Grand, John Last, Sr., John Niemeyer, Benjamin Staal, Anthony Sweetman, Van't Hof, and Nicholas Viss.

On April 29, 1949, the board of trustees accepted the indenture (a legal paper similar to a constitution) formally establishing the CSEF as a bona fide trust-fund type of foundation.

The Christian-textbook program of the NUCS has always been the main concern of the foundation. Its indenture, however, is sufficiently broad to include other elements that "further the interests of Christian education," such as granting scholarships and sponsoring conferences, all in the context of "the Reformed world and life view."[10]

For several years the trustees personally donated monies for a scholarship program for graduate and undergraduate teachers and Christian high-school seniors.

Since its inception the foundation has, upon application by the NUCS board, provided funds for curriculum development. In 1950 the modest figure of $20,000 was granted for specific Christian textbook projects. By 1965, the annual commitment had risen to $41,500. During the early years, in harmony with the scope of the objectives of the foundation, the board of trustees authorized pay-

10. CSEF indenture; see the section about purposes.

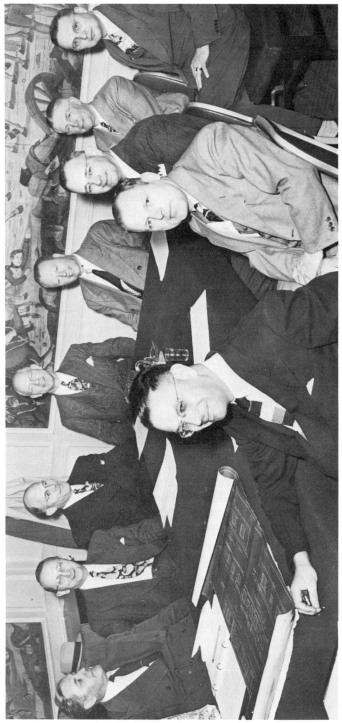

Board of Trustees of the Christian School Educational Foundation. L to r: Jacob Van't Hof, James La Grand, Nicholas Viss, Dr. John Van Bruggen, Dr. George Broodman, Anthony Sweetman, Herman Baker, John Niemeyer, Aldrich Evenhouse, John Last.

ment of one-half of the salaries of the NUCS director and the
promotional secretary. Later, this was simplified by issuing an
administrative grant annually to the NUCS for managing and housing the foundation.

One of the exciting and long-lived modes of gathering funds for
the foundation is Foundation Day, conceived and first promoted
by Heerema. Its design was simply to solicit the money usually
spent on Valentine's Day and encourage the schools to give students an opportunity to contribute that money to the foundation.
Teachers, by and large, turned the challenge into contests, while
using the occasion to fortify convictions for Christian education
in the minds of children and youth. The yield the first year, 1950,
was $4,703. By 1965 the income had climbed to a gratifying sum
of $21,316, and it continues to mount each year.

Although this publication on Christian-school history takes
readers only to 1965, an account of the CSEF would be incomplete
without a short reference to the fact that in 1975 a Canadian
counterpart was established, known as the Canadian Christian
Education Foundation, Inc. (CCEF). It is vigorous, having a national identity in Canada, and wholly committed to the same ideals
and objectives as the CSEF.

There is little doubt that the growing Christian-textbook and
curriculum-development program was possible only with the stable source of income provided by the CSEF and later by the CCEF.

Ongoing Goals Despite Personnel Changes

Like 1943, the year 1953 was marked by many changes. In
March, 1953, Heerema decided to take up a parish ministry and
accepted a call to become the first pastor of the Plymouth Heights
Christian Reformed Church. Shortly thereafter, Van Bruggen accepted an appointment to teach educational psychology and related courses in the education department of Calvin College. To
succeed these men the NUCS board appointed Vander Ark, then
principal of Western Christian High, Hull, Iowa, and Dykstra, principal of West Side Christian School, Holland, Michigan, as director
and assistant to the director respectively. The positions held by
Van Bruggen and Heerema were radically redesigned by the board,
because the board thought that promotion, although having high
priority, could be integrated with the total rapidly expanding pro-

Sidney Dykstra.   John A. Vander Ark.

grams of the NUCS. Vander Ark was made responsible for all
facets of the program. Within this context, Dykstra was mainly
responsible for the educational program.

Neither specialized in curriculum planning, but both learned
quickly and applied themselves to the job at hand. Dykstra explained his view on Christian textbooks in an article in *Christian
Home and School.* He reasoned that textbooks play a prominent
role in education; they make a tremendous impression on youth;
every text has a philosophy of life; not all teachers can compe-
tently bridge the gap between secular texts and Christian teaching;
it is psychologically sound to teach in a positive manner ... and
quarreling with the author on the selection of material and interpretation is an inefficient and ineffective way of spending teaching
opportunities.[11]

The drive for publishing Christian instructional materials, read-
ers will recall, is actually as old as the Christian-school movement.
In each period of NUCS history, people advocated publishing
Christian textbooks. For this period, anchorman Vander Ark des-

11. November, 1954, p. 15.

ignated this facet an educational frontier. In a chapter written for *One Hundred Years in the New World,* the Christian Reformed Church (CRC) centennial book published in 1957, he uses this language to indicate that textbooks reflect the philosophy undergirding Christian schools:

> Our frontier deals with the explication of subject matter, but it is not limited to that. Our purpose is to relate all subject matter to God, the Creator-Redeemer. And, furthermore, in doing this, to seek to form the personalities of the children mindful that they are created in the likeness of God; that is, to lead them toward the fulness of the stature of Christ which is the will of God for all His children.[12]

Making decisions on what Christian textbooks and other teaching aids to publish was and is difficult. Priorities must be spelled out. It was generally agreed that first concerns should be with content, not "drill" subjects, as reading, arithmetic, grammar, and spelling were commonly called. Priorities should be given, the decision-makers concluded, to areas of learning that have strong religious implications, particularly regarding what Christian faith has to do with the study of Bible, history, and areas of learning that make explicit the implications of the Christian faith.

Bible studies have always had top priority, since knowledge of the Bible and one's response to it are basic in education. History and social studies, literature and the fine arts, and natural sciences have also been considered sensitive to Christian interpretation, touching on how God reveals Himself and how Christian character and values are formed through learning.

Sometimes organized bodies within the family of schools took initiative to develop curriculum in a given area. A notable example for this is the work of the Michigan Christian Principals' Club. In the early 1950s it prepared a major part of a new Bible curriculum for the elementary and junior-high grades and submitted these materials to the NUCS for further development and publication.[13] The result was an alternate curriculum that is still extant in the NUCS inventory.

The NUCS had been pressured from time to time by its con-

12. P. 144.
13. The principals doing the work were John Borst, Barney Peterson, John Smilde, John Vanden Bosch, and Mark Vander Ark.

stituents to consider preparing publications dealing with specific topics and subjects. A notable example of this process was in the field of science. A survey on science teaching in Christian schools was made by the NUCS in 1949–1950. The finding was "little uniformity among schools." This prompted the NUCS to study the desirability of publishing a separate graded science series. The conclusion, written by Henry Bengelink and John De Vries after they pondered the responses, was that the NUCS could not afford such an undertaking. The issue drifted for several years; then it was picked up in the 1958 convention under the theme "Christian Education and Science." De Vries, who had served on the original education committee of the NUCS, was the principal speaker. With the announced background statement that science was considered a neglected area in Christian schools, and that available materials were saturated with teachings about evolution, the delegates adopted a resolution urging the NUCS to consider ways and means to meet the challenge. (It should be noted that the entire American educational system was very science-conscious at this time.)

Sometimes major projects have been proposed, investigated thoroughly, postponed, and brought to fruition in a modified format many years later. The preparation of a Christian reader series is a case in point. Since the origin of Christian schools in Anglo-America there has been latent interest in a basic reader series for the elementary grades. It mounted to a ground swell in the years 1956 to 1961. One of the chief proponents at that time was Walter De Jong, who frequently served on the NUCS education committee. He argued, along with other good reasons, that a series for kindergarten through sixth grade would be consistent with plans to have a reader series for the junior-high grades, the Pilot Series in Literature.

The education committee and the staff did much work in planning a series that was well-developed, both pedagogically and in content. The factors, however, that stymied efforts were the difficulty in choosing a method of teaching children to read and the overwhelming cost involved in preparing a series.

Ten years later, in 1965, a literary, not basic, reader was judged a viable option. It was to be called the Sounding Series. It was to emphasize Christian culture rather than the technique of reading, in part because of the absence of a working consensus on the best methods to teach reading.

A significant resolution was adopted at the convention in 1961. It requested the NUCS to consider preparing a year's course in ethics as part of a Bible program. (Gordon Oosterman, who later became a staff member, submitted the resolution.) The reason for such a course was not fully articulated, but the resolution reflected a need for more instruction on ethical and moral choices that students face in life and on what the Bible has to say about current problems. The significance of the resolution was not that it led to immediate production of a publication, but rather that it was a prophetic voice. It called for more attention to teaching Bible from a biblical, theological approach, as contrasted with the more traditional acquisition of Bible knowledge.

Modus Operandi: Problems and Changes

To carry on a responsible Christian-textbook and curriculum-development program, the NUCS has always marshaled the help of many people. In the early years, authors were promised royalties on the sale of published materials. A case in point were the *Pupil Bible Manuals* by Blystra, Fakkema, and Yff. Nonstaff members received a modest royalty on all sales.

As far back as 1946, you will recall, the education committee encouraged the NUCS to accelerate its educational program. The committee had a major role not only in deciding what to publish, but also in selecting authors and supervising the whole process. As an inducement to obtain authors, payment to writers or authors was shifted from royalties to a flat sum.

Members of the education committee, of course, were not reimbursed for their service, only for out-of-pocket expenses. Membership on the education committee required considerable devotion and sacrifice as well as time. There were monthly meetings on Saturdays for a term of three years. The committee painstakingly critiqued all materials written for publication.

The NUCS provided a staff editor who served as advisor to the education committee. Well-deserved tributes must be paid to several editors whose credentials included capacities to discern teachable materials, edit for style and mechanics, and deal with an unwieldy supervisory body. Recognition should be made of Dykstra who, after a few years, chose to pursue graduate studies. Gertrude Borduin, Joyce Pastoor, Tona Huiner, Jacoba Bos, Greta

Rey, John Brondsema, and Gordon DeYoung all had strategic roles in this period. The latter two also served successively as secretary of the education committee. Both exercised special competence in layout, printing, and other facets of book production. All editors worked closely with the education committee. A committee system has both its virtues and its vices, one of the latter being the slow, discouraging aspects of the system that can repeatedly delay a project.

During the period 1962–1965 the education committee introduced some new concepts based on the conviction that writers of curriculum materials ought to be experts in selected fields of teaching. The NUCS made a judgment that as many as three fulltime curriculum consultants could be engaged within three or four years, and that such persons might further qualify themselves by taking relevant courses at a university.[14] Nelle Vander Ark was appointed in 1963 as the first fulltime consultant; her field was language arts. She was granted a brief period at the University of Chicago to prepare for the task. Two years later Henry Triezenberg was appointed to serve as science consultant. He was pursuing a doctoral program at the University of Wisconsin and a starting date was postponed until his goal was realized. Soon after the close of this period, in 1966, Oosterman was appointed as the consultant in social studies. He immediately assumed his duties.

The consultants were given primary responsibility to determine what materials ought to be prepared, with the understanding that curriculum guides ought surely to be written. To facilitate their

John Brondsema
and Gordon De Young.

14. NUCS board of directors minutes, Feb. 21, 1963, article 29.

task and to assure the NUCS and its schools that there was a firm
defense for undertaking what consultants determined ought to be
done, the NUCS board authorized each consultant to select a body
of professional teachers in his or her field to help in the decision-
making process.

During these crucial years, constituents manifested impatience
with the deliberate procedures in publishing Christian textbooks
and with what appeared to be a failure in getting a wider-scale
curriculum-development program under way. In spite of some vac-
illation on methods of operation, the accomplishments were significant. Book three of the Pilot Series in Literature, edited by
Merizon and Haan, was completed. An entire historical Bible-study
series for grades kindergarten through ten was published: *Bible
Curriculum Guide*, kindergarten through third grade, revised by
Brondsema; *My Bible Guide*, grades four through six, by Jessie
Mae and Martha Bruinooge; *Old Testament Studies*, grades seven
and eight, by Edward Bossenbroek; *Ministry of Christ*, grades
eight and nine, and *The Kingdom of God*, grade ten, by Francis
Breisch.

William Hendricks completed two manuscripts at this time: one
for a Christian textbook on government, *Under God*, and a resource unit on sex education, *God's Temples*. For music, Wilma
Vander Baan and Albertha Bratt, with the assistance of Betty
De Vries, prepared *Children's Hymnbook*. Curriculum guides completed were *Music Curriculum Studies* by Vander Baan and *Language Arts Curriculum Guide* by Nelle Vander Ark. *Library Book
Guides* had been published annually since the 1940s. In 1963, a
select reading guide, *Good Reading*, was prepared by a committee
of which Gerda Bos was chairwoman.

The NUCS board, again acting upon the advice of the education
committee, experimented with another route, that of asking for
volunteers to compose teaching or resource units. There were
resolutions at the 1963 and 1964 conventions asking the NUCS to
meet the growing insistence on more curriculum materials through
voluntary effort. A unit on a subject never previously attempted
was received and accepted: *Communism: A Resource Unit for
Christian Schools* by J. Marion Snapper in collaboration with Les-
ter De Koster and M. Howard Reinstra. Snapper was chairman of
the education committee when the 1963 resolution was adopted.
The resource unit reflected his support of volunteerism. A *Book*

of Poetry prepared by Lynden, Washington, Christian-school teachers was prepared under the sponsorship of District 7. Otherwise, the response was poor. Curriculum efforts at best remained spasmodic.

There seemed to inhere in the resolutions and the NUCS decision an impatience with the seemingly slow pace of producing curriculum materials. The education committee voiced its concerted opinion that the better way to go was through properly prepared staff and nonstaff curriculum consultants.

Knowing that it could not afford to hire consultants in every branch of curriculum, the NUCS chose to retain several nonstaff curriculum advisors. This resulted in the appointment of Corrine Kass and Paul Zwier as advisers in reading and mathematics. Serendipity also played a part. In its effort to get service on preparing a curriculum guide in art, which recently gained the status of a regular discipline in Christian schools, not just a Friday-afternoon happy hour, the education committee discovered that Edgar Boevé had thought about this and much more. He had a nearly completed manuscript for a book on the teaching of art. Boevé agreed to be an art advisor to the NUCS and his book was jointly published with Concordia Publishing House. Also at this time, Dennis Hoekstra was engaged as curriculum advisor in Bible.

In addition to appointing and investing in staff members who would specialize in curriculum studies, and enlisting needed curriculum advisors, the NUCS took two other steps to guarantee a wider range of service. It introduced a program of conferences and workshops for teachers in service and decided to appoint a curriculum coordinator. The first NUCS-sponsored curriculum workshop was held in July, 1965, on language arts. Leading NUCS participants were Nelle Vander Ark, Greta Rey, and Sheri Haan.

Curriculum Conference

At the close of this period, a history-making event took place. For the first time since 1943, at the urging of the education committee and the staff, the NUCS agreed to a careful self-examination, especially with a view to long-range planning of educational materials. Like the effort in 1943, a decision was made to get opinions from everyone. Despite occasional changes of autocracy or bureaucracy, the NUCS has tried to stay in reasonably close contact with the thinking of its constituents. A series of questionnaires was prepared and sent to school boards, teachers, principals, ministers, and educational leaders at the college level. That, in itself, was an oblique accomplishment — widespread involvement of many. The point of the opinion polls was to learn from constituents whether they thought the NUCS was truly on a charted course in curriculum planning and publishing or merely drifting. Essentially the responses validated almost all of the goals and programs already envisioned by the NUCS. One message that came through clearly was that a more rapidly paced publication (Christian-textbook) program was urgently desired. The constituents did not emphasize the second step that the NUCS envisioned, namely, conducting programs designed to implement the use of new materials and to assist schools directly to improve instruction.

The year 1965 will long be remembered for the curriculum conference. For too long a period there had been confusion and experimentation in curriculum planning and publication. It was not sufficiently clear to all which way the NUCS was or should be leading.

Sixteen people,[15] representing a cross section of leaders concerned with education, were invited to participate in a two-day, in-depth evaluation of NUCS curriculum development. The conference was held in the pleasant surroundings of Calvin Seminary. The objective of the conference was to get answers to questions such as: What is involved in curriculum development? What resources in persons and money are available? What are the responsibilities of the NUCS, Christian colleges, schools, and professional organizations? The upshot was that the conferees reaffirmed the implementation of a full program of publishing materials for teachers and pupils — including curriculum guides — and the continued acquisition of curriculum consultants or advisors, especially in subject areas where the need is evident and resources permit. The conference strongly advised the NUCS to take the step it initiated to train teachers in the use of new materials and to be ready to assist schools in their efforts to improve

15. Bert Bratt, Calvin Bulthuis, Clarence De Boer, Adeline De Bruyn, Gordon DeYoung, Herman Kok, John Last, Sr., Leslie Plutschouw, Douglas Ribbens, Garrett Rozeboom, John A. Van Bruggen, John Vanden Berg, John A. Vander Ark, Robert Vander Vennen, Marion Vos, and Dorothy Westra.

instruction. The conferees urged Calvin College "to bend every effort to make possible the earning of graduate credit"[16] and asked the NUCS to re-evaluate its graduate scholarship program in the hope that recipients might give some specific service to the NUCS curriculum-improvement program.

The conference also envisioned a staff-oriented curriculum council consisting of coordinators along with both staff and non-staff consultants. By specifying a staff-oriented council the conferees meant to pinpoint the locus of responsible leadership that would make wise corporate decisions. The education committee, for better or worse, was looked upon as superfluous and soon disbanded in favor of a staff-oriented determining body. The committee's importance was realized too late, and eventually another committee with similar duties and a new name came into existence. Committees, like children, are essential in any good educational enterprise; without them there is too little to keep idealistic educators in touch with reality.

16. Calvin College did begin a master of arts in teaching program in 1977.

8

Reflections Apropos for 1965

Twenty-two years may seem like a long time. It isn't; neither are twenty-two years of Christian-school history from 1943 to 1965. During this time, the Christian day-school system changed noticeably. The number of member schools in the National Union of Christian Schools (NUCS) increased from 94 to 272. Pupil population in these schools quadrupled, increasing from fifteen thousand in 1943 to sixty thousand in 1965.

In retrospect, the issues that were prominent in 1943 clearly established the beginning of a period of change. By 1965 new conditions were manifest, giving credence to the year 1965 as an appropriate ending of one epoch and the beginning of another. Distinct changes in educational conditions were discernible in 1965. In Anglo-America, it is generally agreed, the forties were years of sweeping changes; the fifties were generally considered a passive decade; the sixties brought on agitation and further changes.

The term *knowledge explosion* was on every educator's list of "in" words. Books with titles such as *How Children Fail* (John Holt); *Revolution in the Schools* (Ronald Gross and Judith Murphy); *School Curriculum Reform* (John I. Goodlad); and *Transformation of the School* (Lawrence A. Cremin) revealed the extensively critical attitude toward state or provincial school education.

Sterling McMurrin, U.S. Commissioner of Education, in testimony to the Appropiations Committee of the House of Representatives in November, 1961, designated "quality of education" as the number-one target. "Incompetent teachers," he asserted, "were the cause of the problem." "The uncertainties and anxieties of our people in quest for meaningful and purposeful endeavor," he further avowed, "was the spiritual dimension American education faces." Being a man of integrity, the commissioner likely was presenting a disinterested description of affairs as they really were, and not trying to wheedle money out of Congress.

Christian educators took cues from such assessments. "Spiritual life is drifting toward God-effacement. Secular forces are taking the offensive. ... The Christian school, we firmly believe, is the custodian of spiritual values as they relate to our culture."[1]

The concept of value education, interpreted quite differently by two main streams of religious and educational thought, was on the horizon by 1965. The secularists, who disown God's revelation as normative for thinking and doing and who give priority to man's cunning, began to speak of "value clarification." They thought in this vein: Badness in man — also in the child — is a remnant of the beast from which he ascended. Knowledge is power, and knowing *about* values should result in rational choices. If right formulas are applied, goodness and purposeful endeavor will result. Christian educators, on the other hand, insisted on the need to *identify* Christian values and then teach them. In this regard Christian schools basked in a historically-rooted legacy of positive protest.

In the political arena, Christian-school leaders were becoming more adept at helping the public, and particularly public officeholders, properly understand the role of the Christian school and enhance its status at all levels of government.

Representative of this growing concern were several events. In the United States, some representatives of Christian schools, together with NUCS personnel, were invited to the 1965 White House Conference on education. (A few had been invited in 1960.) President Lyndon B. Johnson's provision for aid to education, the Elementary and Secondary Education Act, made a studied attempt to skirt the thorny church-state controversary by aiding the child or the teacher rather than the school. Title II, for example, one of the several components, provided for the permanent lending of library books to private schools. Title III made some aid available

---

1. Director's report, in Christian School *Directory*, 1964, p. 168.

to certain disadvantaged children in either system. Other titles provided funds for teacher-enrichment courses in certain subjects.

Although the benefits of the act to private education were not extensive, this act compelled public-school authorities to recognize the rights and the needs of private schools. Leaders of public and private or Christian schools began to talk together.

The Canadian Scene: 1965

Christian schools continued to grow and increase at a steady pace even though immigration diminished considerably. There was evidence among Canadian Christian schools of both greater reliance on the NUCS and a growing independence from it.

A continuing program of summer courses (begun in 1957) was still conducted in 1965 with fifty teachers in attendance. Teachers in the latter year were R. Kooistra, H. Evan Runner, Paul Schrotenboer, Dorothy Fridsma, Arnold Snoeyink, Rita Van Westenbrugge, and Harold De Jong. Conducting separate summer sessions for Canadian teachers rather than inducing teachers to attend Calvin College was still based on the peculiar need of Canadian teachers.

Albert Hengstman, having recently been appointed as fulltime executive director of the Ontario Alliance of Christian Schools, was the coordinator. The Ontario Alliance and the NUCS together worked out the conditions of his appointment. Ontario was eager to have its own school visiting program. By assigning a part of this service that it subsidized, the NUCS both gave its moral support and agreed to pay a portion of Hengstman's salary for two years.

Christian schools continued to be established in Ontario at a steady pace. In 1965, London District Christian Secondary School and Georgetown District (elementary) School, with Wayne Drost and George Petrusma as principals, were added to the growing list. Toronto District Christian High, having started in 1963, dedicated its new facility in 1965. In the dedicatory ceremony, President F. G. Reinders accepted a scroll that reads, "Unless you serve God with singleness of heart and mind, the school will be a place of darkness."

In 1965, two Canadians were appointed trustees of the trusts that heretofore had no Canadian representatives on their governing boards. Bert Hielema from St. Catharines was appointed to the Christian School Educational Foundation board and Henry Nieman from London to the board of the Christian School Pension Trust Fund.

In Alberta, the Calgary Christian school, having begun operations in temporary quarters in 1963, dedicated a new four-room school building in 1965. Marten Vander Meulen was president and Gerben Vander Veen the principal. Edmonton opened a new junior-high-school building the same year.

Encouraging reports came out of British Columbia. Two schools were in existence on Vancouver Island, Victoria and Duncan. Victoria (now Pacific) closed the school year with a surplus in the treasury. Duncan dedicated a new facility. Syrt Wolters, the first director representing British Columbia (NUCS District 12) on the NUCS board of directors, was the speaker. His address[2] was representative of Canadian thinking on the relevance of Christian schools in Canadian society. "The time has come," he stated, "to answer publicly the questions which always seem to arise on the establishing of Christian schools." Rhetorical questions persisted: Why go to the expense of operating a school when ours is an excellent free system? Why do the Dutch immigrants not accept "our way of life"? Is not separating yourselves undemocratic? Do you not agree that Canadian public education is good? These rhetorical questions gave rise to discussions of substance.

Wolters systematically answered the questions with these familiar themes: God is at the center of life in all aspects; the Christian school will develop the best Canadians; Christian schools *are* democratic in the sense that they are open to children of parents who want them taught in a Christian way. If the government operates a school, it strives for neutrality, which does not suffice to meet the first principle, that God is in the center of all of life.

Curriculum Publications

In the early 1960s the NUCS struggled to find an answer to questions regarding the scope and the sequence as well as the pace of producing curriculum materials. Several units portraying Christian perspectives were published, such as the statement on

---

2. *Christian Home and School*, July-August, 1965, p. 17.

Creation and Evolution by John Brondsema, Jerome De Jong, Martin Wyngarden, Enno Wolthuis, John N. De Vries, Bert Bratt, and John A. Vander Ark. *A Resource Unit on Communism* by J. Marion Snapper and *Foundations of Government* by William Hendricks were issued. Publications were made available in art: *Children's Art and the Christian Teacher* and *50 Symbols of the Christian Faith* by Edgar Boevé, and in the field of music *Hymns for Youth* (1966) compiled by John Hamersma, Wilma Vander Baan, and Albertha Bratt.

Gordon DeYoung was appointed coordinator of publications in 1964, succeeding Brondsema, who had served as writer and editor of educational materials. Given a strong impetus by the 1965 curriculum conference not only to continue a publications program but also to expand and accelerate it, the NUCS pursued this course with new vigor.

The period of engaging fulltime consultants, one of whom was to be designated curriculum coordinator, began. A continentwide accent was first on language arts, then on social studies and science, while other areas such as Bible were not to be neglected. Teachers' guides, such as *Language Arts Teachers Guide in Writing*, were published. Workshops were initiated; for example, the language-arts workshop directed by Donald Oppewal and led by Grace Huitsing, Nelle Vander Ark, and Greta Rey representing the NUCS, and Stanley Wiersma and Bernard Van't Hul representing Calvin College. The Grand Rapids Educators' Club sponsored a workshop in Bible that stimulated the preparation of new pupil manuals. Gordon Oosterman and Henry Triezenberg took up their appointments in 1966 and 1967 to be fulltime consultants in social studies and science respectively. Dennis Hoekstra was engaged as a parttime Bible consultant, as was Paul Zwier for mathematics.

The concept that "doing curriculum" was every school's obligation was popularized. The result was not that the NUCS was expected to do less but more in this area. Plans were laid in this transitional period "to enlarge the [curriculum publication] tent, ... lengthen [its] cords, strengthen [its] stakes" (Isa. 54:2, NIV).[3] The trend of acquiring the services of knowledgeable people in specific areas of curriculum and enabling further professional studies, if necessary, was underway.

3. This was also used as the 1965 convention theme.

Writers such as Harry Blamires influenced Christian educators.[4] Blamires contended that there no longer is a Christian mind. Most of the acclaimed thinkers and critics of our day, he wrote, are humanistic. He than charted a course showing what parts of the Christian mind clash with current world views. The Christian mind, Blamires wrote, has a supernatural orientation, is aware of evil, has a definite conception of truth, an acceptance of authority, and concern for the person — all this in distinction from the secular mind.

The planners of the 1966 Christian-school convention were so impressed by the relevance of Blamires's book that they made the title the theme for the convention.

Wider Vision

The physical voice of an outstanding spokesman for Christian education was silenced when Peter Eldersveld died on October 13, 1965. But that did not terminate his influence. Speaking at the 1948 Christian-school convention, he had prophesied, "We have been almost exclusively introvert in our efforts for Christian education. Now, as we emerge from our linguistic isolation and take our place on the public scene, we are beginning to realize that Christian education is indispensible not only for the building of the church within, but also for the effort of the church without."[5]

Further reading of that address leads one to understand that Eldersveld had two dimensions of "church" in mind. He first had in view the loosening of the unofficial yet effective parochial bond between Christian schools and the Christian Reformed Church, and secondly, the vision to influence a broader Christian public.

With respect to the first group, the Reformed family of schools was being enlarged beyond traditional NUCS communities at this time. Schools were established with nonconventional, yet Reformed, constituencies in Memphis, Tennessee, called the Evangelical Christian School. In Huntsville, Alabama, Westminster Christian Academy began in a Presbyterian setting. Together they gave evidence of a growing sense of a more ecumenical community among Christian schools.

4. Refer to Blamires's *Christian Mind* (London: S. P. C. K., 1963).
5. *Christian School Annual*, 1948, p. 94.

Communications with Christian-school advocates on other continents also became more commonplace. In Kingston, Tasmania (Australia), the Calvin Christian School opened in 1962, the first one "down under." O. J. Hofman, a correspondent of the NUCS, was the headmaster. A second school, Tyndale Christian School, was organized in Blacktown, New South Wales, in 1966.

The NUCS has, since Mark Fakkema's efforts in the forties, shared the experience of operating Christian schools in the Reformed tradition with many inquirers from the non-Reformed sector of evangelicals. The numbers influenced to open Christian schools is not known. No statistical data can be reconstructed, but the effect is evident. To get a proper perspective on the dramatic growth of non-Reformed Christian schools, one must bear in mind that they did not proliferate until after 1965. According to Paul Kienel, executive director of the Association of Christian Schools International, relatively few such schools were in existence in 1950, and in 1977 two new schools per day came into being.

The NUCS became involved in a fellowship of the Protestant school systems in the sixties. In 1963 the NUCS initiated a conference of representatives of bodies that had once before been gathered in a meeting by NUCS invitation back in 1949. Represented in 1963 were the Lutheran Church-Missouri Synod (Frederick Nohl); the American Lutheran Church (Donald Vedder); the National Association of Christian Schools (NACS; John F. Blanchard, Jr.); the Protestant Episcopal Church (Clarence Brickman); a main branch of the Mennonite Church (Clarence Fretz); and the Assemblies of God (Hardy Steinberg). Also in attendance were Brondsema, Philip Elve, Gerald Knol, and John A. Vander Ark, representing the NUCS.

The initial, exploratory conference had an atmosphere of tentativeness. There were nevertheless some tangible results. A better understanding of the nature of each group's efforts in fostering Christian schools was a major accomplishment. This resulted in a willingness to share materials already produced, as well as to inform each other of plans for future publications to serve Christian schools. Joint action on church-state matters surfaced, too, as a likely area for cooperation. Of significance was the consensus to hold meetings of this kind periodically. William Kramer, longtime secretary of parish education of the Lutheran Church-Missouri Synod, Blanchard, and Vander Ark were designated as a steering committee to promote and plan future meetings. In addition to the bodies listed, representatives of the Wisconsin Evangelical Lutheran Synod, Seventh-Day Adventists, and other Mennonite groups were invited. The new conclave, known as the Protestant School Conference, held several conferences between 1963 and 1971, at which time some members of the conference, together with representatives of parochial and independent schools, organized the Council for American Private Education (CAPE). It superseded the loosely organized Protestant School Conference, which then passed from the scene.

In an attempt to make its influence felt on the church "without," to use Eldersveld's language once again, and on the American and Canadian public generally, the NUCS made another effort at this time. It set up a public opinion committee whose task it was to scan written materials for both favorable and unfavorable contents about Christian education and to formulate appropriate responses in widely distributed media. Oppewal, Oosterman, and Walter De Jong worked diligently for a few years but, failing to ignite the enthusiasm of more respondents, the NUCS abandoned the watchdog effort.

NUCS Service Program Enlarged

"The NUCS fundamentally was and is a service organization ... [and] through good and acceptable service has become a leading force in the independent school movement, deftly affecting thinking of administrators, teachers, and boards of Christian schools faced with problems and challenges." So wrote the executive director in his annual report to member schools in 1965.

To carry on a growing service program, the NUCS enlarged its building at 865 Twenty-eighth Street, the first building expansion since 1949. In this transitional period, for example, the NUCS took on the difficult task of evaluating schools as an advisory service. An ad hoc committee consisting of three principals of the Kalamazoo, Michigan, Christian schools (Gerrit Likkel, James Veltkamp, and Ivan Zylstra), at the request of the NUCS, made a study of school visiting and recommended that the NUCS prepare to render that service to schools that requested it. The board engaged Nicholas Yff, a retired principal, to begin the program. Also, teacher placement, a long-time service, became a more demanding one as the system grew. Moreover, school boards asked for specific help not only in setting up schools, but also in promoting and operating continuing schools.

A separate School Relations Department was set up in 1963 and Elve was appointed as the administrator. The secretary who served before, through, and after this period of growth, Dorothy Uiterdyk, was named executive secretary of the department. In 1964, the NUCS held first of many board workshops on promoting Christian schools. In 1965 it conducted a workshop on school-board leadership in Calgary, Alberta. A new service, namely, assessing the readiness of a community to set up a school, was a response to need. Responding to needs of its member schools has long been regarded as the raison d'être of the NUCS.

Service-oriented publications such as *Board Member Handbook* by John Brouwer and Mark and John A. Vander Ark; *Administrator's Teacher Manual* by Elve; and an updated version of *Christian School Standards* were issued during the early 1960s.

Programs grew in number and usefulness in other areas, such as the NUCS-administered financial-security measures. The pension fund and health insurance were prominent among these, and with increased school use they gained momentum. Jennie Druvenga was appointed as executive secretary in this area in 1963.

Changing Patterns in Education

An avalanche of new terms became standard educational jargon at this time. Team teaching, programmed learning, instructional television, ungraded schools, core curriculum, shared time, and teaching the "whole person" (as if there were halves or fourths or sixteenths) were touted as panaceas for educational ills. Some were obvious attempts to overcome deficiencies in existing educational practices. Most were administrative techniques and a few were fundamental philosophic changes in methodology. Christian schools, true to their innate conservatism, were slow to shift from time-tested concepts and careful in adopting changes in the pattern of education. They did, however, embrace some changing patterns. Increased formal teacher education influenced the willingness to accept some change. Approximately 65 percent of the teachers in Christian schools had bachelor's or master's degrees in

Gordon
Oosterman.   Philip Elve.

1965. In the wake of a current stress on being more "humane" in the treatment of children, teachers were elated to remember that such was always the attitude in Christian schools. Nevertheless, they were influenced to be less authoritarian in their treatment of children, reflecting both changing social mores and new insights gained from studies by Christian psychologists. Special education became a more acceptable and available blessing for special children. Schools such as Elim and Children's Retreat received wide acclaim and warm receptions. The larger Christian schools made commendable attempts to meet the needs of children with special problems. Experienced teachers in regular classrooms, for example, Marcia Zwier and John Kamp, were motivated to prepare for positions in special education.

Another indication that Christian schools were coming of age was the awareness that schools should provide for the continuing progression of all learning, duly recognizing a wide variability among children in every aspect of their development. Formal guidance programs gradually became standard provision for Christian high schools, although in many instances not without prodding by accreditation associations and state departments of education. Christian educators have long been providing less formal guidance and hence looked askance at this new formal requirement. Similarly the requirement for driver's training was not kindly received by those who wondered what it had to do with Christian education.

A concern over guidance as a standard function of Christian schools came to expression in a resolution adopted at the 1960 convention. The resolution asked that the NUCS give thorough consideration to the place of guidance in the overall program of Christian education. A five-man committee consisting of Michael Ruiter, Tim Rey, Andrew Ten Harmsel, John Naber, and Gerald

Postma went to work on it. Rey passed away suddenly and Harvey Ribbens took his place on the committee. These men prepared a pamphlet called "Guidance for Christian Schools." The record will show that, once introduced, counseling became a permanent part of many a Christian high school. Larger schools, less personal contact, and the seemingly increased pressures of modern life indicate the timeliness of incorporating this concern into Christian-school programs.

With growing schools and changing times, it comes as no surprise to hear of changing administrative designs at this time. Larger administrative units gained favor, although there was a consensus that bigger was not necessarily better. Sharing public-school facilities, although questioned by many Christian-school leaders who wanted no watering down of all that was to be Christian in a school, was tentatively acceptable to some.

There was in the mid-1960s "the sound of a going in the tops of the mulberry trees" (II Sam. 5:24, KJV) with respect to Christian education. (Harold Dekker, of Calvin Seminary, made appropriate use of that striking scriptural figure of speech in an address on educating for Christian service at the 1960 annual convention in Worthington, Minnesota. It has since been frequently used as characterizing and challenging the onward movement.)

The number of schools and their enrollments were on a steady although less precipitous rise than before 1965. Teacher education was in a stage of being perceptibly upgraded, both in the amount of formal education and in recognition of Christian perspectives in teaching. Although Christian-school administrators were still busy with unresolved problems, they had the satisfaction of knowing about policies and practices that had gone through the crucible of testing. Also by 1965, Christian schools and the NUCS were geared up to build a greater reservoir of learning and teaching materials specifically designed for Christian schools.

The time was at hand to hold a wider vision with respect to who should be interested in Christian schools. The sometimes exclusivistic tendency of the Calvinistic movement was giving way to a greater sense of community. That does not nullify the fact that by and large, the Calvinistic schools, or the Kuyperian schools as they are sometimes called, followed the development of the Christian Reformed Church. The obligation of the Reformed constituency became evident. Joel Nederhood often challenged the

Reformed radio audience with this (paraphrased) expression: What we must do is abundantly clear, given our sensitivities and our theological and educational treasury.

The Reverend Calvin Cummings, minister of the Word in the Orthodox Presbyterian Church, spoke at the dedication in 1963 of the new building of the Wilkinsburg, Pennsylvania, Christian school. He was long-time president of its board of trustees. In his address he reminded his audience that when excavation began, the engineer discovered large deposits of silt where the foundation should rest. To prevent sinking and cracking of the new structure, the silt was removed in order that the foundation might rest on solid shale.

The analogy is obvious and apt. "The Christian school is built, not on the soft, moist silt of the wisdom of men. It is built on the solid rocks of God's changeless truth."[6]

The panorama of living scenes involving thousands for whom Christian education is a principled way of life continues to roll, and the scenes that postdate 1965 must be recaptured in subsequent writings.

6. *Christian Home and School*, September-October, 1963, p. 3.

Appendix A

Doctrinal Statement of the National Association of Christian Schools

1. We believe the Bible to be the inspired, the only infallible, authoritative word of God.
2. We believe that there is one God, eternally existent in three persons: Father, Son, and Holy Spirit.
3. We believe in the deity of our Lord Jesus Christ, in His virgin birth, in His sinless life, in His miracles, in His vicarious and atoning death through His shed blood, in His bodily resurrection, in His ascension to the right hand of the Father, and in His personal return in power and glory.
4. We believe that for the salvation of lost and sinful man regeneration by the Holy Spirit is absolutely essential.
5. We believe in the present ministry of the Holy Spirit by whose indwelling the Christian is enabled to live a godly life.
6. We believe in the resurrection of both the saved and the lost; they that are saved unto the resurrection of life and they that are lost unto the resurrection of damnation.
7. We believe in the spiritual unity of believers in our Lord Jesus Christ.

Author's note: The doctrinal statement of the (former) National Association of Christian Schools is the same as that of the National Association of Evangelicals.

Appendix B

Openings and Closures of Christian Schools

1943	Holland Marsh	ON
	Willow Grove (merged with Philadelphia-Montgomery Chr. High, 1965)	PA
1944	Alameda	CA
	Hanford	CA
	Ontario	CA
	Middletown	PA
1945	Lacombe	AB
	Glendale (became Burbank, 1953; Sun Valley, 1961; closed, 1963)	CA
	Ripon Chr. High	CA
	Lansing (Illiana Chr. High School)	IL
	Ellsworth (Ebenezer)	MI
	Vogel Center	MI
	Prinsburg (Central MN Chr. High)	MN
	Philadelphia N.E. Chr. Day School	PA
	Corpus Christi Presbyterian Day School (resigned, 1947)	TX
	Lynden Chr. High	WA
	Sumas (merged with Lynden, 1973)	WA
1946	Arcadia	CA
	Oskaloosa	IA
	Wellsburg (Timothy)	IA
	Boston (nonmember status)	MA
	Grant	MI
	Bridgeton	NJ
	Vineland	NJ
	West Collingswood (Camden County)	NJ
	West Sayville	NY
	Germantown (joined NUCS, 1952)	PA
	Seattle	WA
1947	Ocheyedan	IA
	De Motte	IN
	Dispatch (closed, 1954)	KS
	East Palmyra	NY
	Kirkwood (closed, 1957)	PA
	Oostburg	WI

1948	San Diego (one-year membership, NUCS)	CA
	Inwood	IA
	Prairie City	IA
	Palos Heights (Elim)	IL
	Goshen	NY
	Sunnyside	WA
	Randolph (Immanuel)	WI
1949	Edmonton (Central)	AB
	Vancouver	BC
	Sibley	IA
	Falmouth (Ebenezer)	MI
	Holland (South Side)	MI
	Muskegon (Western MI Chr. High)	MI
	Hills	MN
	Charlotte (joined NUCS, 1967)	NC
	Rehoboth Chr. High	NM
	Volga	SD
	Waupun	WI
1950	Denver Chr. High	CO
	Ackley	IA
	Grangeville (closed, 1952)	ID
	Lafayette	IN
	Grand Rapids (Adams Street; member NUCS, 1958 – 1960)	MI
	Grand Rapids (Sylvan, extension of Oakdale)	MI
	Chandler	MN
	Holland	MN
	Hollandale	MN
	Worthington	MN

	Flushing (joined NUCS, 1960)	NY
	Bellevue	WA
	Cincinnati (operated one year)	OH
1951	Sioux Center (Lebanon; closed, 1977)	IA
	Ada	MI
	Holland (South Olive)	MI
	Lansing (joined NUCS, 1965)	MI
	Rudyard	MI
	Bigelow	MN
	Cleveland (West Side)	OH
	Portland (West Hills)	OR
	Platte	SD
	Mt. Vernon	WA
	Delavan	WI
1952	Flint	MI
	Imlay City	MI
	Lucas-McBain	MI
	Hamilton (Calvin)	ON
	Seattle (Watson Groen)	WA
1953	Abbotsford	BC
	Elmhurst (Timothy Chr. High)	IL
	Hudsonville (Unity Chr. High)	MI
	New Era	MI
	Walker (merged later with West Side, G.R.)	MI
	Wyoming Park (extension of Southwest, G.R.)	MI
	Monsey (Rockland Co.; closed, 1960)	NY

	Jarvis District	ON		Palos Heights	IL
	Wilkinsburg (Trinity, Pittsburgh, 1976)	PA		Western Springs (Western Suburbs)	IL
	Sarnia	ON		Grandville	MI
1954	Ladner (Delta)	BC		Cleveland (East; closed)	OH
	Artesia (unit of Bellflower)	CA		Drayton (Calvin)	ON
				Trenton	ON
	Hawarden (closed, 1967)	IA		Philadelphia-Montgomery Chr. High	PA
	Leighton (merged with Pella)	IA		Colton (closed 1972)	SD
	G.R. (Children's Retreat)	MI		New Holland (Dakota Chr. High)	SD
	G.R. (Plymouth [Hastings St. 1908]; joined NUCS, 1954)	MI		Monroe	WA
	G.R. (South Chr. High)	MI	1957	Edmonton (West)	AB
	Manhattan Chr. High	MT		Tucson (closed, 1964)	AZ
	Gallup (closed, 1963)	NM		Lulu Island (now Richmond)	BC
	Aylmer (Immanuel)	ON		Newton	IA
	Salt Lake City (closed, 1975)	UT		Oak Lawn	IL
1955	Edmonton (East)	AB		Borculo	MI
	Langley (Shannon Heights)	BC		Dearborn	MI
				Lamont	MI
	New Westminster (now Burnaby, John Knox)	BC		Bowmanville (John Knox)	ON
	Ft. Lauderdale	FL		Chatham (Calvin)	ON
	Dutton	MI		Hamilton (District Chr. High)	ON
	G.R. Godwin (Immanuel; merged with Calvin, S.W.)	MI		Kenosha (closed, 1970)	WI
	G.R. Millbrook	MI		Waupun (Central WI Chr. High)	WI
	Springdale (merged later with Holland Marsh)	ON	1958	Bellflower (Elim, now Salem)	CA
	Strathroy (Calvin)	ON		Lake Worth	FL
1956	Maple Ridge (Haney-Pittmeadow)	BC		Miami (Southern; closed, 1961)	FL
	Kanawha	IA		Battle Creek	MI

	G.R. (West Side added a unit at Highland Hills)	MI		1961	Smithers (Canadian)	BC
					Escondido (Calvin)	CA
	Highland (merged with Lucas-McBain)	MI			Miami (Westminster; succeeded Southern)	FL
	Holland (Maplewood)	MI			Minneapolis (Calvin)	MN
	Holland (Rose Park)	MI			Dundas (Calvin)	ON
	Sussex	NJ			Fruitland (John Knox Memorial)	ON
	Rexdale (Timothy)	ON			Guelph (Calvin)	ON
	Wellandport	ON			London (Parental)	ON
	Wyoming (John Knox)	ON			St. Thomas (Ebenezer)	ON
	Sioux Falls (Calvin)	SD			Wallaceburg (Calvin)	ON
1959	Phoenix	AZ			Seattle (Riverton; resigned membership, 1964)	WA
	Hayward (Brookhaven; NUCS, 1962 – 1964)	CA		1962	Lethbridge (Immanuel)	AB
	Ontario Chr. High	CA			Houston	BC
	San Jose	CA			St. Petersburg (Southern Keswick; NUCS 1965 – 1968)	FL
	Denver (Van Dellen)	CO				
	Wyckoff (Eastern Chr. Sch. Assoc.)	NJ			Canaan	ME
	Brampton (John Knox)	ON			Bowmanville (Dunham Chr. High)	ON
	Brockville (John Knox)	ON			Burlington (John Calvin; NUCS, 1965 – 1966)	ON
	Clarkson (Mississauga-John Knox)	ON			Clinton & District	ON
	St. Catharines (Calvin Memorial)	ON			Ft. William (Thunder Bay)	ON
	Willowdale	ON			Oshawa (Emmanuel)	ON
	Woodstock (John Knox)	ON		1963	Calgary	AB
1960	Duncan	BC			Sioux City (Morningside; resigned membership, 1970)	IA
	Victoria (Pacific)	BC				
	Bradenton	FL			Barrie (Timothy)	ON
	Winnipeg (Calvin)	MB			Brantford	ON
	Silver Springs (Washington, D.C.)	MD			Kingston (Calvin)	ON
	Shelton (Timothy; NUCS, 1964 – 1965)	NJ			Williamsburg (Timothy)	ON
	Athens	ON				

	Woodbridge (Toronto Dist. Chr. High)	ON	
1964	Agassiz	BC	
	Surrey (Frazer Valley Chr. High)	BC	
	Orange City (Unity Chr. High)	IA	
	Des Plaines	IL	
	Tampa Seminole (joined NUCS, 1976)	FL	
	Shreveport (Baptist Chr. Academy; resigned membership, 1966)	LA	
	Grandville (Calvin Chr. High)	MI	
	Holland (East View — Van Raalte bldg.)	MI	
	Belleville District	ON	
	Burlington (Trinity)	ON	
	Etobicoke (Grace, branch of Rexdale; merged, 1966)	ON	
	Milwaukee (Brookfield)	WI	
1965	Huntsville (Westminster Chr. Academy)	AL	
	Orlando	FL	
	Rock Valley (Hope Haven)	IA	
	Dover (American)	NJ	
	Georgetown District	ON	
	London District (Christian Secondary)	ON	
	Cordova-Memphis (Evangelical)	TN	

Appendix C

Significant U. S. Supreme Court Decisions (1943 to 1965) Relating to Christian Schools

1943   West Virginia Board of Education v. Barnette, 319 U. S. 624, 87 L. Ed. 1628, 63 S. Ct. 1178. The court ruled that the state statute requiring that students salute the flag was unconstitutional, based on the premise that although the state has the (limited) power to standardize education, it does not have the right to impose a uniform system of beliefs and values on all students.

1944   Prince v. Massachusetts, 321 U. S. 158, 64 S. Ct. 438, 88 L. Ed. 645. This decision echoed that of the landmark case Pierce v. Society of Sisters, 268 U. S. 510, 45 S. Ct. 571, 69 L. Ed. 1070 (1925), which struck down an Oregon law requiring all children to attend only public schools for state-mandated education.

1947   Everson v. Board of Education, 330 U. S. 1, 67 S. Ct. 504, 91 L. Ed. 711. The court permitted state payments to reimburse parents of parochial-school students for the cost of bus transportation.

1948   McCollum v. Board of Education, 333 U. S. 203, 68 S. Ct. 461, 92 L. Ed. 649. The decision declared "released time" unconstitutional where religious groups could use public-school facilities and time to instruct students of their faith in principles (doctrines) of that religion.

1952   Zorach v. Clauson, 343 U. S. 306, 82 S. Ct. 679, 96 L. Ed. 954. The court allowed "dismissed time"; that is, the Supreme Court ruled that instruction given by religious groups during school hours at various religious centers was permissible, provided attendance was not compulsory.

1954 Brown v. Board of Education, 347 U. S. 483, 74 S. Ct. 686, 98 L. Ed.
      873. The court emphasized that applying the First and Fourteenth
      Amendments to educational legislation, education, and the acqui-
      sition of knowledge is a fundamental liberty.

1962 Engel v. Vitale, 370 U. S. 421, 82 S. Ct. 1261, 8 L. Ed. 2d 601. The
      court outlawed the voluntary use of a prayer composed by the
      New York Board of Regents.

1963 Schempp et al. v. School District of Abington, 374 U. S. 203, 83
      S. Ct. 1560, 10 L. Ed. 2d 844. The court held that the Pennsylvania
      law that provided for the reading of at least ten verses of the
      Holy Bible, without comment, at the opening of each day was
      unconstitutional.

For a comprehensive report on U. S. Supreme Court cases regarding education and also an authoritative discourse on government/school relations, refer to Gordon Spykman et al., *Society, State, and Schools: A Case
for Structural and Confessional Pluralism* (Grand Rapids: Eerdmans,
1981).

Bibliography

Books and Dissertations

Blamires, Harry. *The Christian Mind.* London: S. P. C. K., 1963.

Cremin, Lawrence A. *The Transformation of the School.* New York: Alfred A. Knopf, 1961.

De Jong, Norman. *Christianity and Democracy.* Nutley, NJ: Craig Press, 1978. Abridged version of unpublished dissertation, "Boyd H. Bode: A Study of the Relationship Between the Kingdom of God and Democracy," University of Iowa, 1972.

De Jong, P. Y. *Christian Education in a Changing World. Story of the Schools.* Hamilton: *The Christian School Herald,* 1962 and 1964.

De Kruyter, Arthur H. "The Reformed Christian Day School Movement in North America." Unpublished thesis, Princeton Theological Seminary, 1952.

Gaebelein, Frank E. *Christian Education in a Democracy.* The report of the NAE committee. New York: Oxford University Press, 1951.

Kranendonk, Dick L. *Christian Day Schools Why and How.* St. Catharines, ON: Paideia Press, 1978.

Kraushaar, Otto F. *American Nonpublic Schools: Patterns of Diversity.* Baltimore: John Hopkins, 1972.

_____. *Private Schools: From the Puritans to the Present.* Bloomington, IN: The Phi Delta Kappa Educational Foundation, 1976.

Ludwig, J. B. "Control and Financing of Private Education in Alberta: The Role of Parents, the Church, and the State." Unpublished thesis, University of Alberta, Edmonton, 1970.

187

Mc Garry, David D., and Ward, Leo. *Educational Freedom and the Case for Government Aid to Students in Independent Schools.* Milwaukee: Bruce, 1966.

Oppewal, Donald. *The Roots of the Calvinistic Day School Movement.* Calvin College monograph series. Grand Rapids: Calvin College, 1963.

Oosterman, Gordon, et al. *To Find a Better Life: Aspects of Dutch Immigration to Canada and United States, 1920–1970.* Grand Rapids: CSI, 1975.

Phillips, Charles E. *The Development of Education in Canada.* Toronto: W. J. Gage, 1957.

Spykman, Gordon, et al. *Society, State, and Schools: A Case for Structural and Confessional Pluralism.* Grand Rapids: Eerdmans, 1981.

Stob, George. "The Christian Reformed Church and Her Schools." Thesis, Princeton Theological Seminary, 1955. Ann Arbor: University of Michigan Microfilm, 1974.

Thayer, V. T. *Formative Ideas in American Education: From the Colonial Period to the Present.* New York and Toronto: Dodd, Mead, 1965.

Yearbooks, Magazines, and Journals

Christian School Annual, published by the National Union of Christian Schools (now CSI), 1922–1960.

Christian School Directory, from 1961 to the present.

Christian Home and School, official organ of the CSI since March, 1922.

Christian School Herald, published under the sponsorship of Ontario Alliance of Christian Schools from 1957 to 1971.

Christian Educators Journal, published by Christian Educators Journal Association since 1961.

Calvinist Contact, K. Knight Publishing Limited, St. Catharines, ON.

Curricular Theory

Beversluis, N. Henry. *Christian Philosophy of Education.* Grand Rapids: CSI, 1971.

De Boer, Peter P. "Some Significant Shifts in Curricular Theory for Calvinist Colleges and Day Schools." Unpublished paper, 1982.

Steensma, Geraldine, and Van Brummelen, Harro, editors. *Shaping School Curriculum, a Biblical View.* Terre Haute, IN: Signal, 1977.

Triezenberg, Henry, et. al. *Principles to Practice,* Grand Rapids: CSI, 1979.

Wolterstorff, Nicholas. *Educating for Responsible Action.* Grand Rapids: CSI, 1980.